"Challenging, authentic and practical... in this book Lindsey reminds us that whether transforming leaders, teams or whole organisations, it is the individual that is at the heart of the change process. This insight, among many others comes directly from Lindsey's experience with her clients and she has few peers as a practitioner in the field."

Richard Lucas - Director,
Pricewaterhouse Coopers Consulting

"Too few books can be said to have been written by a double expert. Lindsey not only has an impressive knowledge of NLP but she also has a wealth of experience in changing business whilst working in a major international consultancy company. Put the two together and you have the recipe for this must-have book for anyone who wants to get ahead, stay ahead and truly be a leader in business."

Robert Smith, Master Trainer of NLP

"Lindsey Agness is an inspiring teacher with a wealth of experience in managing change across a number of diverse blue chip companies. Her book 'Change your Business with NLP' is destined to become a business textbook for companies of all sizes especially in today's testing economic climate.... I would recommend her book highly if you want to know how to stay in front of your competition, and get the very best out of your business, this book is a must."

Sandra Wheatley, Senior Internal
Audit Manager, Transport for London

All it takes, at times, are the right words uttered in a specific way & energised with that special something. I had such an experience during a corporate change management workshop run by Lindsey. This culminated in my making a radical career shift which, in turn, resulted in the building of a profitable $500M+ business. I've grown substantially from every encounter with Lindsey. You never just meet her. Lots of stuff is going on inside you moving you towards your goal, ~~~~~ ~~~~~ wards. You'll feel the

D1144118

you, guiding you towards your goals. You don't get to escape from yourself with Lindsey coaching you. She is the master at bringing about reconciliation between your dreams & the necessary actions for success."

Jim Nicholas, Microcontrollers Division General Manager at ST Microelectronics

"In 1997 Lindsey attended my NLP Practitioner Certification, 13 years later she is a member of my NLP Master Trainer Programme. The highest level of certification in the field! This stands testimony to her relentless development of herself. I believe NLP is one of the absolute best tools for creating business success available today. And *Change Your Business With NLP* is one of the best books to give you the tools to make it really happen for you."

David Shephard, Certified Master Trainer of NLP, Founder of The Performance Partnership and President of The American Board of NLP.

"A practical, creative book to achieving the results you want in your business using Neuro Linguistic Programming techniques. Lindsey's clear and concise writing style provides a book with easy-to-follow exercises and reflections to which the reader can return time and again."

Dr Julie Hodges, Director of FT MBA Programme at Durham Business School

"Universities face challenging times ahead and departments and faculties will need to become agile and impact driven if they are to increase their competitiveness. Lindsey offers tools and techniques that focus on implementing transformational change and achieving measurable benefits. Having worked with Lindsey on an organisational change project, I have no doubt that this book will stimulate ideas for enhancing opportunities for growth in an increasingly tough financial environment."

Dr Sue Colley, Director of Employer Engagement and Enterprise, Faculty of Health Sciences, University of Southampton

Change Your Business
with NLP

Change Your Business with NLP

Powerful Tools to Improve Your Organisation's Performance and Get Results

Lindsey Agness

CAPSTONE
be inspired!
™

Library of Congress Cataloging-in-Publication Data

Agness, Lindsey.
    Change your business with NLP : powerful tools to improve your organisation's performance and get results / Lindsey Agness.
        p. cm.
    Includes index.
        ISBN 978-1-907312-40-3 (pbk.)
    1. Neurolinguistic programming.   2. Leadership.   3. Management.
4. Organizational change. I. Title.

    BF637.N46A35 2010
    658.4'063–dc22

                                                                    2010028563

Set in 10/14 Meridien Roman by Aptara
Printed in [Great Britain] by TJ International Ltd, Padstow, Cornwall

This book is dedicated to my children, Sophie and Oliver, to help them in their future careers, and to my mother who always encouraged me to succeed in business.

Contents

Introduction: Why is NLP important for business?

The most important question you should ask yourself as you consider reading this book is 'Am I getting the results that I want in business?' As you consider that question, notice what comes into your mind. For example, do you want to improve your own results as a leader, build an exceptional team, change the rules of the game or culture of your organisation or transform your customer relationships? Maybe you would benefit from developing your skills in all of these areas. If you found yourself answering 'yes' to any of these questions then I guarantee that you will get immense value from this book.

In a tough market, Neuro-Linguistic Programming (NLP) techniques can be applied to the challenges that today's leaders face – identifying and delivering efficiencies, holding onto clients in the midst of increased competition, improving morale and increasing organisational performance. NLP changes mindsets, focusing and motivating you into a positive state of self-belief, thereby empowering you to face your challenges head-on and transforming the business you are in.

The essential aim of this book is to introduce you to specific NLP tools and techniques in the context of real business issues and to show you how to apply them through a series of pragmatic exercises, case studies and evaluations. I will demonstrate through the evidence base of the case studies that NLP does indeed deliver measurable results to business.

Who is this book for?

My own field of research and application is 'People Development' in business. Primarily, therefore, this book is for:

- Middle to senior leaders in business (including those who aspire to these positions) who have the authority and influence to make changes using NLP tools and techniques and who want to make a measurable difference to their organisations

- People development or HR professionals including consultants, trainers and coaches who want an understanding of how to use NLP to create improved results for their clients

- NLP practitioners (by practitioners I mean anyone qualified in NLP) who want ideas and recommendations about how they can apply the tools they have learned in business

- Potential buyers of NLP who wish to understand more about its application and evidence before they invest time and money in NLP-based services.

This book is designed to deliver better results in any type of business from global corporation to public sector organisation. If you work in the public or charitable sectors you may find the label of 'business' unfamiliar. The definition I discovered from Wikipedia described a business as a:

'legally recognised organisation designed to provide goods and/or services to customers. Most are privately owned and formed to earn profit that will increase the wealth of its owners and grow the business itself. Businesses can also include cooperative enterprises, not-for-profit or be state-owned.'

So when I use the term 'business' I use it in its widest sense. I know from personal experience that NLP tools and techniques work equally well across this whole spectrum of organisations.

The book is designed as a journey of discovery where you, the reader, will learn through practical application of the exercises. For you to get maximum value from the experience I urge you to apply each exercise to your own personal situation, whether you are already a leader, an aspiring leader, a people development specialist, NLP practitioner or potential buyer of NLP services.

Where are you and your business now?

Any change process should start with reflection on where you are now. It's rather like putting a stake in the ground which you come to at the end of the journey to discover how far you have travelled. I learned this when I worked as a change management consultant for one of the top global consulting firms. I was taught to always start a project with the end in mind. It was important to work with our customers to define the outcomes and associated business benefits they would gain from working on the project with us. They understandably wanted measurable results from our work and so it became essential to set a baseline of where they were at the start of the project to make it easier to measure their success at the end. I view this book as a change project, in that it is designed to transform you and your business. Therefore, it's important to know where you are at the start of this journey. With that in mind, I invite you to complete the following quiz of discovery. The quiz follows the structure of the book and is relatively light-hearted so please be honest with your answers.

//

Exercise 1: The Business Discovery Quiz

Part 1: Transforming Leaders with NLP

1. Do you have compelling goals for your future?
   a. Absolutely
   b. Yes, but you're not that committed to them
   c. No, you just go with the flow

2. When something isn't working do you:
   a. Do whatever it takes to sort it out
   b. Keep your fingers crossed that it will go away
   c. Keep your head down and blame others

3. When you get feedback about your leadership skills do your staff say:
   a. They are totally inspired by working with you
   b. They point out a number of areas where you could improve
   c. They feel lost and directionless

Part 2: Transforming Teams with NLP

4. What makes a world-class team?
   a. Shared vision and values
   b. Focus on the customer
   c. Making the numbers no matter what

5. How do you encourage creativity in your team?
   a. By setting specific time aside as a team to generate new ideas
   b. By listening to team members when they come up with ideas
   c. I don't as we are fighting too many fires each day

6. When was the last time you had a courageous conversation with a team member?
   a. In the last month
   b. In the last 6 months
   c. Can't remember

Part 3: Transforming Organisations with NLP

7. What's most important when starting an organisational change project?
    a. Clear business case with defined benefits
    b. Support for the project
    c. Keeping everyone happy
8. How do you successfully implement a culture change?
    a. Change the reward system
    b. Crank up the communications
    c. Let the 'old guard' manage the process to keep the peace
9. What's the biggest challenge of a remote team?
    a. Poor communication
    b. In-fighting
    c. Time-wasters

Part 4: Transforming Client Relationships with NLP

10. What's most important for building long-term client relationships?
    a. Excellent rapport
    b. Good products
    c. Expense account

11. What's the best tip for a new presenter?
    a. Just be themselves
    b. Advise them to use Powerpoint slides so they don't get lost
    c. Have a script they can read to ensure they cover everything

12. How would your clients describe your business?
    a. Consistently exceeds their expectations
    b. Consistently meets their expectations
    c. Consistently fails to meet their expectations

Now, add up the number of As, Bs and Cs you have scored, and find out what your choices suggest about you.

Mostly As. Congratulations! You made some excellent choices that demonstrate that you and your business are already moving in the direction of the **Brilliant Zone**. I'll show you how you can both become world-class.

Mostly Bs. Not bad but you and your business are becoming complacent and there's a danger you'll get stuck in the **Grey Zone**. It's time to take action and I'll help you develop some ideas to do just that.

Mostly Cs. Good job you picked up this book as you are like a ship without a rudder – directionless and making poor choices which will prevent you from steering a more successful course. Get ready for a rough ride as you face up to the changes you need to make to move out of the **Awful Zone**. I'll show you how.

What is NLP?

For those of you who are wondering what NLP is all about, now's your chance to find out more and to understand why I've chosen it as the technology of change used in this book.

NLP, or Neuro-Linguistic Programming, has proved a challenge to define neatly. Tosey and Mathison describe it as 'a kind of reverse engineering, applied to human capabilities'.

That's because in the early 1970s, a linguist, John Grinder, and a mathematician, Richard Bandler, studied individuals who were excellent communicators and technicians of change. They started by asking a question: 'What makes the difference between *world-class* and *mediocre* performance?' They observed many world-class performers, including famous therapists, and discovered the beliefs, mindset and strategies which delivered their success. They explored both personal and professional example of successful change to discover the tools and techniques that delivered fast and sustainable results. As a result, they formalised their change techniques under the name 'Neuro-Linguistic Programming', known as NLP, to symbolise the relationship between the brain, language and the body and the results that can be achieved. Tosey and Mathison made the point that:

> 'NLP does not invent these patterns; it identifies them, strips them down to their essentials, sometimes refining and re-packaging them and makes them available for others to learn... it is a way of coding and reproducing excellence that enables you to consistently achieve the results that you want.'

NLP is very eclectic in that it draws from many diverse fields of practice. In his book, *Whispering in the Wind*, Grinder described NLP as having:

> '...spread like wild-fire throughout the world... It [NLP] works across cultures, generations, age groups and fields of application. There are now hundreds of thousands of people in the world whose lives have been profoundly and positively impacted by the application of this patterning called NLP.'

Why has it been so successful? Unlike other approaches that tell you **what** you need to do, NLP is a **how to** technology. It tells and shows you **how to** be the leader you want to be, have the business success you want to have and spend your time doing the things you really want to do. For most people things happen and they react unconsciously out of their awareness. NLP offers a better way. It gives you the tools to react differently by choice, to be more aware of your thoughts, feelings and behaviour. You are then ready to take responsibility for your results in all areas of your life, not only your business life.

Let's look at each element of NLP in turn and I'll explain what it's all about.

Neuro

Neuro is all about what we **think** – or our thoughts.

Neuro means 'what goes on inside our heads'. We have over 60,000 thoughts a day. These form our internal world of pictures, sounds and feelings. It is these conversations, dialogues or arguments we have with ourselves in our thinking process that drive how we feel, our mood and ultimately how we respond to events. In NLP terms these are called our **internal representations**. For example, if you have an important meeting with your boss coming up and you think about it going badly, this in turn is likely to make you feel bad. Guess what? With those circumstances, you're likely to create exactly what you are thinking about inside your head. On the other hand, you can focus on the meeting going well and feeling very excited about it. Guess what? You're much more likely to create it going well for yourself. To be clear about the importance of this, your thoughts and the way you feel will **impact directly** on the success of the meeting.

The critical point to realise is that we can control our thoughts and I will show you how.

Linguistic

Linguistic is all about what we **say**, both verbally and non-verbally.

Language determines how we communicate with other people and ourselves. It is how we label our experiences and much more. Empowering language generates empowered behaviour. Likewise, negative language limits our choices.

It is estimated that 93% of communication is non-verbal. This means how you say what you say (intonation, volume, speed, etc.) carries five times more information than the words spoken. And how you use your body (gestures, facial expressions, posture) is even more influential. As our thoughts and feelings literally 'leak' out of us through our bodies, consider what yours say about you? For example, when you are getting ready for an important meeting, are you focused on getting the result you want or do you let your anxieties get the better of you? Does your physiology in that situation portray nervousness and concern or someone who has confidence and knows what they want?

Programming

Programming is all about what we **do**.

We are all running programmes in our minds, all of the time. These programmes drive the way we behave, our performance and, ultimately, our results. For example, in your career, maybe you notice the same challenges keep showing up? Perhaps you always encounter a difficult boss or maybe you experience conflict in every team that you manage? In these situations, the only common denominator is **you**! These programmes run at an unconscious level in the nervous system which is why they are difficult to change. NLP helps to identify these negative programmes and to change them so these experiences no longer show up in your life. As you think about it now, do you have any scenarios like this?

To bring it altogether, NLP symbolises the relationship between the brain, language and the body. It describes how what we say, think and do interplay and affect our body and our behaviour and our results. As Sue Knight explains in her book, *NLP at Work*, 'It's the difference that makes the difference in business'.

How NLP is used in this book

When I first discovered NLP in 1997, I experienced it as the most results-focused technology I had ever come across (and I'd come across a few having been a consultant for many years!). NLP is all about consistent long-term results that can be achieved fast. In this book you will learn how to use NLP to:

- Develop a 'winning state of mind'
- Dare to be different!
- Improve your leadership skills to inspire and motivate others
- Build a high performing team
- Motivate and engage with staff
- Create innovative solutions to challenges
- Have courageous conversations
- Manage benefits-driven change programmes
- Understand the 'rules of the game' to change culture
- Utilise world-class communication skills
- Quickly build strong rapport and solid business relationships
- Learn how to differentiate yourself with your clients
- Become a relaxed and excellent presenter
- Consistently exceed your client's expectations

What does NLP mean for your business? Positive results will be immediately recognised through increased motivation, confidence and skills. Longer-term benefits include elevated performance and productivity, higher morale and motivation, reduced turnover, lower absenteeism and a higher return on investment.

What's different about this book?

When I was researching NLP books for business, I made an interesting discovery. There seemed to be very few – if any – 'how to' books that showed the reader how specifically to utilise NLP tools and techniques in a pragmatic way in business. Many of the books seemed to over-complicate the subject, making it inaccessible to most business people coming to NLP for the first time. Also, many started from the perspective of the NLP techniques, for example 'anchoring or rapport techniques', without clearly showing how these could be used in different business situations.

This book is different because it turns the traditional NLP business book on its head and asks how NLP can help solve business challenges in today's environment. For example, it shows how to use NLP tools and techniques to build a high-performing team and develop long-term customer relationships. It also offers a range of case studies that demonstrate how NLP has been used and the measurable benefits of doing so. Finally, there are close to 50 pragmatic exercises running as a common theme throughout the book. They provide you with the opportunity to practise your new skills as you learn about the subject matter. It's been proven that knowledge alone does not easily embed in the nervous system to change behaviour. By practising these techniques you integrate the learning for yourself and prove to yourself that you can do it, thereby creating new beliefs about your own competency levels.

The exercises are an essential component of this book. I encourage you to complete them as fully as possible as they will literally take your performance to the next level. You can complete them in this book or, if you prefer, copy them into a personal journal.

I find that there are three ways that people learn. Firstly, you may find yourself enjoying the learning and using the exercises to make new discoveries about yourself. You relish every opportunity to improve yourself and your business. That's the best way to experience this process. Secondly, you may feel some resistance to what you are learning as it challenges the way you have always gone about things. When you feel resistance you know that you are on the verge of learning something important. It's even more important in these moments to stick with the process and the exercises and not skip on to the next section. It will be in one of these specific moments that you discover the most important message for yourself. Thirdly, you may even feel some pain when you realise how 'stuck' you may have become in the 'old' methods you have been using at work and with yourself. In these moments, it's most important of all to keep going. These are the 'moments of truth' for you, moments when you can make a decision about changing the way you do things permanently. I am here to assist you through these moments, to help you understand the new choices you have been given and how best to use them.

Who am I?

I have been using NLP in my corporate work since the late 1990s. I qualified as a trainer of NLP in 2000 and worked as a change management consultant with a global consulting house between 1994 and 2005. Prior to that I worked as a senior manager in local government. In 2005, I set up my own business, The Change Corporation, which focuses on transformational change to help both individuals and businesses achieve their full potential. The focus is on three key areas:

- **Corporate:** working with companies to develop leaders and to deliver benefits from large-scale change programmes
- **Public:** running NLP programmes to assist individuals create permanent change in their lives

- **Coaching:** offering individuals Executive and Break-Through coaching sessions to achieve measurable results

The Change Corporation recently reached the finals in the 'Kent New Business of the Year Award' and I was a finalist twice for 'Entrepreneur of the Year Award'. Believing that it's never too late to develop myself, I started to write in my mid-40s and my first book, *Change Your Life with NLP*, was in the top 20 of all best-selling self-help books in the UK in 2009 (*The Bookseller*, 2009).

I tell you this as I believe I am well-qualified to work with you on the subject of business change. I have used NLP explicitly with my corporate clients since the late 1990s. Because of my background as a consultant and entrepreneur, I'm fortunate enough to have worked in many large businesses, in both the private and public sectors. I've learned what makes the difference and I now want to share that with you.

This book contains a range of case studies, showing how NLP can be used at work. The case studies drill down into specific detail about how it can be used in business and the types of measurable benefits that can be achieved. One of the criticisms often made of NLP is that it is over-sold and under-tested. This book provides important evidence to the challengers of NLP.

How this book works

I've put together a four-part model for this book that focuses on the key areas for change in today's climate. In this tough market, each of the four parts is full of NLP techniques that can be applied to the challenges that you face today – leading with enthusiasm, increasing team performance, changing culture, and holding on to clients in the face of fierce competition.

The four-part model

Part 1: Transforming Leaders with NLP	Part 2: Transforming Teams with NLP
Building strategies for success	Constructing high-performing teams
A winning state of mind	Encouraging creativity in your team
Modelling world-class performance	Having courageous conversations
Part 3: Transforming Organisations with NLP	**Part 4: Transforming Customer Service with NLP**
Managing change effectively	Influencing with integrity
Changing the rules of the game	Powerful presentations
Developing global organisations	Exceeding customer expectations

This book looks through the lens at each of these four themes and then asks, 'How can NLP be used to achieve world-class success in each?' It's a very pragmatic approach that builds from the individual as a leader, to managing high-performing teams, to running an organisation and finishes with delivering world-class customer service. You can pick and mix what you need for your own personal development or choose to work step by step through all the four stages of success.

Use of NLP

NLP was once defined to me as an Attitude of Mind, a Methodology, and a series of Techniques. In this book I've selected 33 core elements from NLP and utilised them across the chapters. Some of them might be described as an Attitude of Mind, some a Methodology and others Techniques. I'm not going to get hung up on which element fits into which category. What is important is that, to maximise your learning, I've included as many core elements of NLP as I can. I've drawn these elements from both the Practitioner and Master Practitioner curriculum so in many ways this book gives you an excellent insight into the methodology, tools and techniques that you would study if you were to take the NLP Practitioner and Master Practitioner Certifications.

I show in Appendix 1 on the NLP grid a summary of all the NLP elements used in this book and where they feature. It's important to realise that these elements are not exclusive to the subjects where they have been used. For example, although I've featured 'Goal Setting' in Chapter 1 'Strategies for Success', the advice and techniques could also be applied in a number of chapters such as Chapter 4, 'Constructing High-performing Teams', and so on. I've made a choice to feature each element only once to avoid duplication and have given suggestions about where else you might utilise that new area of knowledge and skills.

Let's get started

Now I've explained the background behind the book and what it will do, it's time for you to take the first step on your journey. Imagine turning the clock forward one year. You are a successful leader in your business. What do you see yourself wearing? What do you hear yourself saying? And, most importantly, what does it feel like to be that successful? Others ask to model you to discover how it is possible to get the results that you do. Your staff are creative, open and coach each other to achieve world-class results. And in your industry your teams are recognised as the ones to emulate and have won numerous awards. Your organisation culture is aligned to your business strategy and supports the delivery of world-class results. Finally, your customers praise you for continually exceeding their expectations in the quality of service that you provide and your client churn rate is the lowest in the industry. What if that was a description of you and your business?

I have a question for you:

'Are you prepared to step up to what you really can achieve in your business? To be the leader you deserve to be whatever it takes?'

If so, read on...

PART ONE

TRANSFORMING LEADERS WITH NLP

1
BUILDING STRATEGIES FOR SUCCESS

///

As we start this new decade we are still in the midst of one of the biggest recessions of all time. Why are some businesses still growing whilst others are struggling or even going bankrupt? Why are some public or charitable businesses using their funds more effectively whilst others are wasting potential opportunities for efficiencies? One of the key factors is that the businesses that are successful have leaders with a mindset that 'makes things happen'.

These leaders:

- Have a Vision

- Start with the big picture or the end in mind

- Have a healthy appetite towards risk

- Are driven by the need to make a difference

- Are tenacious when things don't go to plan

- Know 100% about their business

- Are passionate

- Innovate

- Most importantly, they are leaders or participants and not followers or spectators

Those organisations with leaders who batten down the hatches and hope for the best may find that, when this storm is over, they have been surpassed by their competitors who were prepared to continue 'making things happen' and learning even through the tough times.

In this first part of the book, we are going to explore exactly where you are starting from – your current mindset, leadership style and the feedback you've received in the past. Then we'll move on to create what you want for the future, setting your personal leadership goals and giving you the tools to develop your own mindset for success.

Where are you now?

Cast your mind back to the quiz that you completed at the start of this book. Were your scores mainly As, Bs or Cs? I described the As as being on the way to the Brilliant Zone, the Bs hovering dangerously close to the Grey Zone and the Cs struggling to move out of the Awful Zone. I'd like to describe these in more detail so you can work out where exactly you sit.

The Personal Leadership Grid

The Personal Leadership Grid describes three personal leadership zones that people typically find themselves in along with the attached generalised experiences. By 'personal leadership' I mean the amount of control and responsibility you are taking currently in order to become the leader you want to be, have the impact that you want to have and achieve the results that you know you are capable of achieving. You don't even have to be a leader right now. The important question is, 'Are you personally leading yourself towards where you want to be?'

Personal Leadership Grid

The **Awful Zone** is a place where you don't want to stay for too long. You feel wretched and unhappy. Normally you find yourself there because something has happened – maybe you've been made redundant, fired or pressurised into a situation that you don't want to be in. The only good thing about the Awful Zone is that it does make you take action and change.

The **Grey Zone** is that place where people all too often get stuck, under-achieving or marking time in careers where they meant to stay for a stop-gap and spent a lifetime instead. It feels comfortably uncomfortable as you know that you are selling out on your potential. I believe that many people spend most of their career in this zone.

The **Brilliant Zone** is the caretaker of our ambitions and dreams. It's the zone where you know you're heading towards achieving your goals. It feels good to be on that road.

The question is: where are you right now?

Exercise 2: Where am I on the Personal Leadership Grid?

Take a red pen and mark where you think you are on the Personal Leadership Grid. Be honest with yourself. As you look at the Grid are you surprised where you ended up? Are you ready to find out how to move faster towards the Brilliant Zone, or how to finally find the courage to move out of the Grey Zone, or how to make an immediate improvement by moving out of the Awful Zone? Good, so let's get started by discovering more about each Zone and how to move up as quickly as possible.

The Awful Zone

The Awful Zone is not somewhere you want to be for long. You end up in the Awful Zone when something significant and negative happens to you such as:

- A sudden redundancy (especially if there is not a pay-off)

- A new boss who treats you badly, maybe even bullies you

- Restructuring where you are left in a role that you don't want

- Withdrawal of funds or budget cuts

- Someone at work who makes your life a misery

- Disciplinary or sacking offence

Get the idea? The Awful Zone is the point of no return. This is the point where you finally take action. It's the moment when you deal with the situation at work differently or you leave. At this point, although it is bizarre to describe it as such, the event does you a favour as it drives you to take action and produce different results. This is the terrain of the Awful Zone.

Claire: the moment of truth

Claire was a senior executive officer working for a central government department. When her boss left she thought long and hard about going for the promotion as she had been encouraged to do by a number of other senior officers in the department. However, she was pregnant with her first child and decided that it would be too much change all at once. She went off on maternity leave and returned six months later with a new boss in post. Her new boss was male, younger than her with much less experience. Instead of working collaboratively with her, he was competitive and stand-offish from the start. He would criticise everything she did whilst at the same time over-loading her with his own work. He also demanded that she work very long hours which was a strain for her with a young baby. Claire tried talking to him and changing her strategies. She began saying 'no' to his demands for her to take on his work and attempted to get her work–life balance back. As a result, their relationship further deteriorated. In desperation, she took out a grievance in the hope that his actions would be fully investigated. However, ranks closed, and, after twenty years of blemish-free service, she negotiated a compromise agreement and left. Though firmly in the Awful Zone, she had the space to re-think her future career. She set herself some new goals to get her career back on track. Having an exciting vision that she was passionate about helped her to take the initial challenging steps forwards.

If you are in the Awful Zone right now this book will give you the tools to resolve the situation or make a quick exit and to begin to move towards what you are really capable of achieving in your career.

The Grey Zone

Everyone knows of someone who feels like they've wasted years at work in a job they don't enjoy and are under-achieving their full potential. Perhaps that's how you feel yourself. Instead of being excited and stretched, you've spent years being bored and miserable. How does this happen?

Often it's because of the promise of something coming in the future, like a final salary scheme pension or the potential of a generous redundancy. This wouldn't be so bad if these 'carrots' were imminent, i.e. within 18 months to two years, but people waste their best years at work waiting for future redemption. I was recently coaching a public sector female manager who was in her early 40s. She was clearly miserable in her role and capable of far more but there were no opportunities coming up where she worked. When I challenged her about why she stayed in a role that made her feel that way she told me she was 'coasting to retirement' and didn't want to risk losing her pension. As she had at least 20 years to her retirement I wondered what her attitude would cost her in terms of her health and self-esteem.

If it's not because of the future, for many it's because of responsibilities they have in the now. For example, a mortgage to pay, family to look after or fear of change can all keep you stuck in a career that you don't really want to be in. I'm not promoting being reckless with your career – we've just experienced a long and hard recession where it can be sensible to sit it out. Yet even the recession can become an excuse for staying stuck. The recession won't last forever and there are many people who have taken risks at this time and done well because not many others are!

I describe the Grey Zone as a place where many people spend their entire careers – it's not awful but it's certainly not brilliant. It's comfortable because it's what they know. Sometimes I describe it as that 'comfortable yet uncomfortable' place. It's uncomfortable because, deep down, people know they are selling out on their ambitions for a 'safe' existence. Over my years of coaching and training I've come to realise that many people settle for second best because they haven't got the courage to do anything about changing their situation. There's a saying: 'If you always do what you've always done you always get what you've always got.' That's the mantra of those who live their lives in the Grey Zone. Life in the Grey Zone feels familiar, comfortable, unfulfilling and stuck, and those in the Grey Zone do not feel they have any choice but to remain where they are. Of course if you are happy in the Grey Zone that's great and I suspect you aren't as you're reading this book!

Jonny: cleaning his career away

Jonny had taken over his father's very successful family cleaning business and had been running it for many years. The business had grown over the years to employ over 100 people and now had some very large corporate contracts and healthy profits. The business funded a good lifestyle – a large home, flash cars, motorbike, lots of holidays. Jonny had been feeling bored and disillusioned for some time yet was scared of admitting it to anyone, especially himself. He found the business very routine as he knew it inside out. Even the thrill of winning new contracts didn't have the same excitement as it used to. He was dragged along to a personal development weekend by some friends and learned that he could make other choices for himself. That was a shock to him. He started to read more self-help books and he got into NLP. Through his personal development training he began to come up with new goals for himself which included a new career as a life-coach. He came right to the edge of making different choices for himself. Yet he still stopped short of making the change, which was very frustrating for him. He was terrified of losing the lifestyle he had built up and of handing over the management of the business to others. He chose to remain in the Grey Zone. I still see him and ask him how he's getting on. He says things like 'not bad' or 'could be better' and then turns away, embarrassed to hold my gaze for too long. What a waste...

There are many people out there in the Grey Zone because they are in careers that their parents or partners chose for them. That's fine if they really want to do that for themselves but too often they follow more out of respect and tradition than excitement and passion. As Jonny discovered, once there, it's a challenge to get out. And, yet it's always possible. I'll show you how.

The Brilliant Zone

You know if you are heading in the direction of the business Brilliant Zone because you have personal and business goals and ambitions. You know what you want to achieve and you're taking action, moving towards your goals and it feels exciting, motivating, exhilarating and stretching. Our best moments are when our bodies and/or our minds are stretched to their limits to achieve something challenging and worthwhile. These are the experiences that you take responsibility for and make happen.

Those with courage, determination and focus move towards the business Brilliant Zone. You can achieve this too. What really makes the difference? These are the people with exciting strategies for success and goals for the future. They are totally focused on their goals and failing is not an option. They never say 'I can't'. Instead, they say 'why not'! You can probably think of a number of successful business people who have this philosophy in life. One of my own personal development strategies is to say 'yes' whenever I'm asked to do something new, as long as it will move me towards my goals, and to worry about it later. Last week it was a request for me to go on live Australian breakfast TV to talk about how to achieve your goals! That was an amazing learning experience.

My story

I spent many years in the Grey Zone, although it might have looked to others as if I had the perfect career. I worked as a change management consultant for one of the top global consulting houses. I was the one in the team who focused on the 'people' side of change when a new IT system was being implemented or business processes being re-engineered. My career wasn't awful – in fact, it was well paid, I learned my trade as a change consultant and I got to travel round the world. But it still wasn't my dream. The hours were long and the increasing time away from home meant that I was apart most weeks from my young family and husband. I felt out of control. I was firmly stuck in the Grey Zone. Then, in the late 1990s something happened that was to change my whole life and begin to move me towards the Brilliant Zone. I did my first NLP training course. It completely blew me away. At the end of the course I had goals for the first time in my life, I felt motivated, believed I had choices and

I wanted to discover what I was really capable of achieving in my career. On my return to work I began to develop my vision of having my own company and I worked on a strategy to get the ball rolling. Through NLP, I'd learned to focus on what I wanted to achieve, take 100% responsibility for my career and create what I wanted without allowing myself to listen to my own excuses about all the 'problems' that might get in the way! I started with small steps; focusing on getting the funding together to do my next NLP training. That's one thing you learn early on in NLP – that the most successful people always have the next goal in mind. The next year I did my Master Practitioner Training and later my Trainer's Training. Now everything was in place.

One of the reasons why people are comfortable in the Grey Zone is that they have never experienced anything different. I knew by the end of my NLP Trainer's Training that the Brilliant Zone existed. It was too late for me to unlearn it and I was determined to get there and stay there. The excitement that I experienced as I began to develop my business was like nothing I'd ever experienced before. I felt alive for the first time in years – maybe for the first time in my adult life. I enjoyed waking up and going to work as each day took me closer to my goal. I wondered how I would ever know enough to run my own business.

Through my NLP training I came across 'Heisenberg's principle'. This states that 100% certainty doesn't exist. Successful business people take risks because they accept that they will never know everything they need to know. The strategy they adopt is 'acting as if' they do know and taking the plunge. This is the equivalent of training your brain to believe you can do something or that you have something already. For example, take a promotion that you want for yourself. Consider how you would behave differently if you had achieved it already. Perhaps you would be more confident and offer to take on additional responsibilities. How would your appearance change? Maybe you would smarten yourself up a bit. Would you sound different? Maybe you would change your tonality to sound more commanding. What would it feel like to have that promotion? All these changes work on two levels – first of all, your colleagues and boss will notice that you are behaving differently, and second, you start to train your own brain that you can do it. This will have the effect of convincing yourself that you can do it so that next time the promotion comes up you'll really go for it and get it.

Your Personal Leadership Model

Your position on the Personal Leadership Grid represents in part where you are now in terms of your Personal Leadership Model. Clearly, those moving towards the Brilliant Zone display strong self-leadership characteristics. They demonstrate the 'making it happen' mindset as they are more likely to be focused, determined and going for it. Those in the Grey Zone have a leadership model of avoidance. They are keeping their heads down and hoping for the best. They are not the movers and shakers of tomorrow (not yet anyway). Those in the Awful Zone have some choices to make and this can kick-start a different success strategy for the future. Of course, these are generalisations and you may or may not recognise these traits as true to you. So, let's add some more detail about how you've led yourself and others up until now.

///

Exercise 3: What's my style?

This exercise explores feedback you've had in the past from your managers and staff about your Personal Leadership Style. If you're not yet a leader of staff use your own self-awareness about 'You' to answer the questions or go and ask some of your colleagues to give you their views about 'You'.

Below you'll find a list of characteristics or behaviours.

Step 1: Circle those behaviours that you've been described as demonstrating in the past – both positive and negative across all three columns:

List A	List B	List C
Focused	Conservative	In denial
'Can-do' attitude	Cooperative	Undemanding
Driving	Hesitant	Suspicious
Collaborative	Low-key	Pessimistic
Pioneering	Cautious	Moody
Determined	Modest	Critical
Competitive	Mild	Evasive
Decisive	Agreeable	Worrisome
Inquisitive	Peaceful	Dependent
Risk-taker	Unobtrusive	Exacting
Responsible	Reflective	Neat
Strong-willed	Sceptical	Negative
Inspiring	Logical	Non-political
Magnetic	Relaxed	Over-trusting
Enthusiastic	Resistant to change	Incisive
Convincing	Non-demonstrative	Hyper-tense
Polished	Passive	Unsystematic
Persuasive	Predictable	Arbitrary
Warm	Consistent	Careless
Action-taker	Deliberate	Unbending
Sociable	Steady	Obstinate
Creative	Stable	Resistant
Total:	**Total:**	**Total:**

Now total up how many behaviours you've circled in each list. Did you score highest in list A, B or C? Generally, you'll notice that list A aligns to Brilliant Zone behaviours or behaviours that move you towards your goals. List B aligns to Grey Zone behaviours or behaviours that keep you stuck. List C aligns to Awful Zone behaviours or behaviours that can lead to a negative outcome.

Step 2: Now list below the positive behaviours you already demonstrate that will assist you to move towards the Brilliant Zone.

Step 3: Now list below the negative behaviours that will hold you back.

Step 4: Now list below the behaviours you want to develop.

Step 5: Summarise below in a few sentences your strengths as a leader and the areas that you want to change and why. If you're not yet in a leadership role, write down below the characteristics you'd like to develop as a leader and the areas of your current style that you'd most like to change.

My strengths as a leader/characteristics I'd like to develop

Behaviours I'd like to change and why

///

Now I'll show you how to develop these behaviours through the Personal Leadership Vision and goals that you set for yourself.

Your Personal Leadership Vision (PLV)

One of the key differentiators to transforming your leadership style is to know where you are going, to have a Personal Leadership Vision and clear goals that will deliver that Vision. Tosey and Mathison argue that a common application of NLP in business is:

'Designing and refining outcomes, ranging from broad visions to very specific goals, and understanding the resources needed to achieve them ... this emphasis of paying attention to future outcomes, and how they are to be achieved is characteristic of NLP.'

I always begin any development process with the outcome in mind as this keeps you focused on and motivated towards your goals.

'Begin with the end in mind'

This is also one of Stephen Covey's 7 Habits of Effective People: 'The *end* represents the *purpose* of your life'. Until you can say what that purpose is, you cannot direct your life in the manner that would bring you the greatest satisfaction. There are no short-cuts here. You need to have a Personal Leadership Vision and habitually set goals that move you towards that Vision. This is important, as your level of excitement and drive about your future comes from your Personal Leadership Vision. It's what gets you out of bed in the mornings and keeps you going when the going gets tough. You begin by finding a Vision for your future that truly inspires you. Every day I remind myself of my own PLV to leave a legacy through my writing, my training events and my coaching that gives many thousands of people more choices about how to improve their performance and the potential success they can achieve. Even though our PLV can seem overwhelmingly stretching and impossible at times, it gives us a purpose for our lives. This section is all about assisting you to develop your own PLV and understanding how your business career is a channel for you to achieve it.

Now you're ready to move on to develop your own PLV, the first question for you to consider is what is the most important thing you want to achieve in your business life? All great leaders have a vision and focus – you know that already. Sir Richard Branson wrote that one of his big goals in life is to live life to the full. This is reflected in the size and scope of some of his projects, for example, Virgin Galactic to drive down the costs of space travel. At this point, don't confuse your PLV with the strategic vision of the organisation you are currently working for. A strategic vision is all about planning and positioning your business. Your PLV is for you. It will, however, assist you to decide if you are focusing and working in the right industry and in the right role. For example, if my legacy is to give large numbers of people more choices about how they lead their lives, I need to be working in an environment that will help me to achieve that. Being a CEO of a manufacturing business, for example, is unlikely to rock my boat. Your PLV will become your framework for making value-based decisions. It will enable you to say 'yes' to good opportunities and decisions and to know what to avoid. Accepting opportunities, however tempting, that divert you from your core focus will usually take up more of your time than you had anticipated and may jeopardise other opportunities that would move you closer to your PLV. It will also help you to communicate a very clear message to others that there is uniformity of purpose and clear goals surrounding everything you do.

So what's your PLV? Sometimes it's easier to think about it in terms of what you would do if you knew it would be an absolute success. Put all the potential issues and excuses to one side for a moment. If you had a plain piece of paper and you could choose anything you wanted, what would it be? If you still have any doubts, the next exercise will help you get to absolute clarity.

Exercise 4: Your Personal Leadership Vision

This process will take about an hour so make sure you have enough time to do it justice and do it in one sitting. Do it alone to ensure that you don't end up with someone else's vision! This exercise is used with permission and adapted from a similar process called 'My Purpose in Life' by David Shephard, NLP Master Trainer. (The original came from *Trusting Yourself* by Sidney Walker.)

Step 1 – My internal drive inventory

First of all you need to work out what really excites and inspires you to take action. Go through the following lists of words and circle all the items that give you a strong positive feeling about what your PLV would mean to you.

Then go back and pick the top three or four themes that have the greatest meaning and importance to you in your business life. There are no correct answers and the meaning of each word or phrase is up to you.

Personal achievement	Leaving a legacy
Winning	Fully expressing yourself
Happiness	Seeking adventure
Developing others	Becoming an expert
Earning lots of money	Power
Building something	Authority
Being liked	Making a positive difference
Gaining approval of others	Prestige and status
Gaining recognition	Developing people
Popularity	Developing things
Creating something	Increasing effectiveness
Being world-class	Seeing how much you can get away with
Getting things done	Trusting others
Independence	Doing a good job
Being your best	Taking risks
Reaching your potential	Being different and still fitting in
Finding excitement	Being unique
Having fun	Controlling
Learning	Being a leader
Gaining wisdom	Having influence over others
Working hard	Making a worthwhile contribution
Gaining mastery	Experiencing life to its fullest

If a word or phrase comes to mind that isn't on the list please add it.

Step 2 – My internal drive history

Now list at least one accomplishment that you achieved in each age range listed below that gave you the greatest sense of joy. These are accomplishments that you personally felt good about regardless of what others thought at the time. They are also accomplishments that showed some leadership potential, no matter how small it might seem looking back. For example, any time in your life where you have been put in charge of something, no matter how insignificant it seemed at the time, or when you have taken the initiative to set something up from scratch. If you can't think of anything, pass on to the next age range. Stop when you reach your current age range.

- 0–12 ....
- 13–17 ....
- 18–22 ....
- 23–30 ....
- 31–40 ....
- 41–50 ....
- 51–60 ....

- 60+ ....

Step 3 – Questions and answers

After you have completed the above, please answer the following questions.

1. Throughout your life, what activity has consistently produced the greatest sense of joy and self-fulfilment for you?

2. What else is important to you about your life?

3. What skills or abilities do you most like to perform?

4. What do you most like about yourself?

5. What patterns, trends or similarities do you observe in all your answers so far in the context of business?

Step 4 - What's your PLV?

Using the answer to Question 5, create a set of words that you feel totally motivated about. The key is to come up with a definite theme that best describes the driving force behind your business life and that provides you with a strong emotional charge each time you read it. Getting your PLV right will give you confidence: a 'feel good' awareness that works. It should be motivational and informative – and it should convey the same message to everyone you meet. Aim for no more than 50 words

For example, my PLV is:

'I am a leader in the development field. My writing, training and coaching develops leaders not followers and acts as a catalyst for change in individuals and organisations. I assist them to move out of the Grey Zone towards the Brilliant Zone and to perform at their highest levels of potential.' 50 words

How was that? As you look at your statement, how do you feel? If you do not feel totally compelled to take action, go back through the previous steps until you come up with a PLV you are happy with and that really motivates you.

Now you're going to bring your PLV alive by making it more specific and by setting goals to help you take the first steps towards achieving it.

Questions to achieve your Personal Leadership Vision

If I were to ask you if you've ever had outcomes in the past that you've achieved I've got a feeling you'd say 'yes'. And if I asked you if you've ever had outcomes in the past that you've not achieved, I've got a feeling that you'd also say 'yes'. So, what makes the difference between the two? Maybe your outcome was just not compelling enough. The important question, then, is 'how can we consistently achieve our vision, outcomes or goals?'

You learned earlier that working with broad visions to specific goals and how they are to be achieved is at the heart of NLP. The NLP method of refining goals or outcomes uses the Well-Formed Outcomes process to produce a thorough, carefully refined and unambiguous outcome. The exercise below uses a set of six questions modified from the Well Formed Outcomes process. During this exercise, it is very important to write the answers down because once you commit the details of your outcome to paper it becomes much more real.

///

Exercise 5: Outcome defining questions

	Question	Purpose
1	What do you want?	Checks that your PLV is stated clearly and positively
2	How will you know when you have achieved your PLV?	Checks your evidence criteria

3	For what purpose do you want this PLV?	Checks that it is compelling
4	What resources do you need to be able to achieve this PLV? What do you need to do to achieve this PLV? Is this PLV something which you, yourself, can achieve? Or does it require that **other** people behave in a certain way?	Checks you have control of your outcome
5	What are the advantages of achieving this PLV? What are the disadvantages of achieving this PLV? What will achieving this PLV lose you?	Checks what you will gain and lose from your outcome
6	What's important to you about achieving this PLV? What will this PLV help you avoid feeling? What is the benefit of this PLV for you and others?	Checks your level of motivation

It takes about 25 minutes to go through the exercise and, ideally, you need a partner to ask you the questions. Get him or her to ask the questions clearly and to assist you through the process as quickly as possible. Ask them to write down your answers and give them to you after the exercise.

What did you notice happening to your PLV as you went through that process? Most people find that it becomes much clearer and they feel more committed towards it. Question 5 is also very interesting because it flushes out what is called 'secondary gain' in NLP. It asks you to think about what you will lose as well as gain when you get your Vision. For example, my PLV required me to leave my corporate career and set up my own business. That required me to change my lifestyle for a while until the business was on its feet. It's very important that consequences are acknowledged and addressed because any internal conflict can cause you to give less than 100% commitment to your PLV and you may end up compromising or even sabotaging your own success.

Your Personal Leadership Goals (PLGs)

Let's now move on to the goals that will help you to achieve your PLV. Experts estimate that only 5–10% of people bother to think about their goals regularly, and only 1–3% have clear written goals. You'll now spend some time clarifying what goals you need to move you towards your PLV and the Brilliant Zone. Your PLV is all-encompassing and sets your direction for the future. The goals that will deliver that Vision for you need to be much more specific. The well-known SMART principles are not NLP but I use them as they are the best way I have found to develop PLGs in ways that mean they are much easier to achieve. Below I briefly recap on what this acronym means.

You should make sure your goal is very **Specific**. For example, instead of setting a vague goal to improve the performance of your team, set a specific goal to improve each key performance indicator (KPI) that your team is responsible for delivering by 25% in the next 12 months.

Secondly, make sure it is **Measurable**. For example, choose a goal with measurable progress, so you can see the change occur. The goal above is measurable as it shows the specific target to be measured, i.e. all KPIs to increase by 25% in 12 months.

Thirdly, make sure it is **Achievable**. This means that it is possible for you. For example, 'I want to become CEO where I work within 5 years' is achievable because there is a CEO and you work there! In NLP we also talk about 'acting as if' we already have our goal as that convinces our unconscious mind that it is possible for you. That's why visualization is so powerful in coaching.

Fourthly, qualify the achievable by making sure it is **Realistic** for you. For example, if you are a year off retirement, becoming CEO may not be realistic. Set the bar high enough to find out what you are capable of but not so high that you will frustrate yourself if you never get there. Focus on the inspirational, not the sensible!

Finally, set a clear **Time** frame for your goal: for next week, in three months, a year, five years, etc – whatever fits with your goal. Putting an end point on your goal gives you a clear target to work towards. Without a time limit, there's no urgency to start taking action now. The following exercise gets you to set clear timescales.

Exercise 6: Your Personal Leadership Goals

Step 1 – Define your goals

Go back to your Personal Leadership Vision. What timescale are you going to set against the achievement of your Vision: 1 year, 3 years, 5 years, 10 years, longer? Once you have the timescale settled, ask yourself what goals you would need to set yourself over that timescale to enable you to achieve your Vision. Imagine turning the clock forward to the point when you have achieved your PLV and look back to now. What will you have achieved by then? What goals do you need to set yourself that will deliver that success? Brainstorm with yourself for now. Make sure they are SMART goals.

One tip. Use present tense language for your goals. It's important to behave as if you already have your goal as this gives your neurology the impression that it's real. Your brain doesn't actually know the difference between what's real and what's imagined.

Step 2 – Work out your plan

This example is my own plan to reach my PLV. I've set it over the next three years: "I am a leader in the development field. My writing, training and coaching develops leaders not followers and acts as a catalyst for change in individuals and organisations. I assist them to move out of the Grey Zone towards the Brilliant Zone to perform at their highest levels of potential."

I coach my clients to work out the final step that guarantees they have achieved their goal and then to work backwards from there. If your goal is more short or long term than this example, adjust the stages accordingly. Take your goals and set them out in your own plan and notice how good you feel as it begins to come alive for you.

Three years

- I am the author of six books across the personal and business development field. Each book builds on the sales of the previous book and together they have already sold 250,000 copies. All of them are in the list of top 20 self-help books in the UK.
- I have built a successful associate team of 50 trainers and coaches within The Change Corporation which delivers NLP and corporate courses world-wide.
- I am franchising Age with Attitude on a world-wide basis and delivering the programme three times a year to groups of over 100 mid-life women.
- I have my own TV show which features self-help for mid-life women.
- The business continues to grow 25% in turnover and net profit year on year.
- I am spending three months of the year in my apartment in the sun!

Two years

- I publish my fifth book.
- I write my sixth book.
- Books 1, 2 and 3 jointly sell 150,000 copies and are all on best-seller listings.
- Books are now selling in America, Australia, India and South Africa.
- Books are translated into a minimum of three other languages.

Eighteen months

- My four books generate a minimum of 10 radio and TV interviews.
- My Age with Attitude programme is running three times a year with groups of 40+ women.
- I have an associate team of trainers of up to 20 people.
- We win 12 more new corporate contracts.
- I write a proposal for my sixth book and have it accepted by a global publisher.
- I write my fifth book.

Within 1 year

- My second book is on at least two best-seller listings.
- My third book is published.
- My proposal for a fifth book is successfully submitted to a global publisher.
- The revised version of *Change Your Life with NLP* is published New Year 2011.
- I appoint a General Manager to The Change Corporation to assist me to build the business.
- We win six more corporate contracts.
- I build an associate team of 12 trainers and coaches.
- I appear in at least three speaker events to audiences of over 100 people.

Within six months

- I publish my second book, *Still 25 Inside*.
- I edit my third book with the publisher.
- I launch the second Age with Attitude programme.
- I win two more new corporate contracts.
- I build my associate team to six trainers and coaches.

Within three months

- I complete my current writing project.
- I win two new corporate contracts.
- I build my brand by writing articles for three national magazines and I'm on TV at least once.

Get the idea! Now it's your turn.

Step 3 – Now write your plan below

Step 4 – Have you done enough?

Before you move on, take another look at your goals and ask if you've really stretched yourself enough. Ask if your goals in your plan will get you to your PLV and check if you've missed anything. Maybe you've discovered you could get to your PLV faster than you thought at first. It's also likely that you'll then need to develop a plan in a similar way for all your goals. For example, I would plan how specifically I was going to complete my current writing project in the next three months.

///

Pulling it all together

I'd like to finish this chapter with a few tips on what else really makes the difference to help you achieve your PLV. I call these the Principles of Success and I've adapted them from traditional NLP.

Principle No. 1 – Get clear on your personal leadership vision and goals

Revisit your PLV and goals. Double check that they really motivate you and that you're totally clear on what you need to do to get there. Now focus on what you want to achieve. Whatever you put your attention to in your life will grow stronger.

Principle No. 2 – Know why it is a must

What are your reasons for wanting to achieve this PLV? Ask yourself, 'If I don't do this now, what will it ultimately cost me?' Make sure that your PLV is for you and that you're not achieving it for anyone else.

Principle No. 3 – Take massive action

Are you prepared to do whatever it takes to achieve your PLV, including things you do not want to do? Re-visit your Personal Leadership Goals and your plan. Challenge yourself by asking if you are prepared to take 100% responsibility in order to achieve your goals. Because, to the extent that you do not, you are giving your personal power away. The only good thing is that you'll always have someone to blame!

Principle No. 4 – Know what you are getting

Be very aware of what works and what doesn't. Ask for feedback, and constantly evaluate your approach. Think of feedback as a gift and remember to learn from any action that doesn't go quite to plan.

Principle No. 5 – Be prepared to change your approach

You must be prepared to be flexible and have a healthy attitude to risk. If what you are doing isn't working, do something different. Don't spend too long wasting your efforts on the same old strategies if they aren't working any more. When you experience uncertainty remind yourself that you are on the right track. And, remember that if you become too fixated on how to achieve your goal you shut out a whole range of possibilities.

Principle No. 6 – Ask for help from those who are already successful

When making major life changes, the most successful people in life model those who have already 'done it'. They do this by going on courses, being coached or simply asking for advice. You will probably find that, with the appropriate support, you will find the process of change more enjoyable and your chances of success will be greatly increased. I cover much more about this in Chapter 3, Modelling world-class performance.

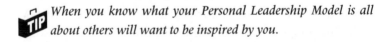 *When you know what your Personal Leadership Model is all about others will want to be inspired by you.*

2

A WINNING STATE OF MIND

///

What is it that really makes the difference? What makes one leader *world-class* and another *mediocre*? This is the question that perplexed Richard Bandler and John Grinder, the creators of the body of knowledge we know as NLP. They made it their life's work to discover the answers. One of the ways they went about doing this was to find world-class models of excellence and to find out how they did what they did. A key finding can be described as the 'Mindset for Success'. World-class leaders do not have fewer problems than less successful leaders, but they *do* deal with problems in a different way. It's not 'luck' that separates world-class leaders from the rest of the pack; they have a very deliberate way of thinking and behaving. It is this that makes the difference. The good news is that we can learn how they think and behave differently.

Now that you have your personal leadership model, vision and goals in place, you are going to explore how to develop a 'winning state of mind' that will help you keep your focus even when the going starts to get tough. There's no doubt that NLP gives us a different lens through which to perceive the world. This can be empowering for leaders and also those who you interact with. Although NLP is sometimes criticised for a lack of theory, many practitioners would argue that its theoretical base is a set of core principles called 'pre-suppositions' that are intended to act as a set of empowering beliefs to assist NLPers achieve the results they want in their lives. They are like the foundation stones of the NLP body of knowledge and I use them as one my company's key differentiators.

Living the pre-suppositions of NLP

One of the curious things about the pre-suppositions is that there is no definitive set published by Bandler and Grinder. Rather, they emerged as principles that underlie NLP and were made explicit by other NLP developers such as Robert Dilts. Because of that, you will find variations within the literature and this book is no different! According to Toser and Mathison, few of the pre-suppositions seem to be original creations of NLP; many came from other fields such as cybernetics. I have utilised various of these principles in business settings over the years in leadership training, coaching and facilitation scenarios. What I show here are those twelve principles that my clients have told me have had the biggest impact on them in terms of transforming their leadership practice. I have translated the language into business-speak with business examples.

Principle	What it means	So what?
Everyone has a different model of the world.	The people you work with will have different points of view to you. It doesn't mean they are wrong and you are right.	It helps you to understand and accept difference in others. It also helps you to understand what might motivate or drive others.

(Continued)

Principle	What it means	So what?
	For example, if I want a member of staff to work overtime to get an order out to a client and they would rather leave on time and go home to their family, who is right?	It doesn't mean you have to agree with that difference.
The meaning of your communication is the response you get.	Your communication with others is only successful if it gets you the result that you intended. For example, if I ask a member of my team to write a report for me and what they produce is not what I expected, whose issue is it? From an NLP perspective, I have not communicated what I wanted in a way that they could understand.	It makes you review the approach taken to communication and encourages you to become more flexible in your style. So, if one approach doesn't work you do something different until you get the outcome you want.
There is no failure, only feedback.	You learn from all of your experiences. For example, if I make an important presentation and it does not go well I can either beat myself up about it or ask myself what I could learn from that experience. Staff learn more from developmental feedback than criticism.	If you interpret mistakes as failures, you feel defeated. If you interpret mistakes as learning opportunities, you continue to develop and have more choice. You should welcome feedback.

(*Continued*)

Principle	What it means	So what?
People do the best they can with the re-sources they have at the time.	People do the best you can with what they know at that time. For example, if one of my team implements a new procedure incorrectly, I know that they did their best at the time. They didn't make a mis-take deliberately.	When you act you make the best choice you can with every-thing you know in that moment. Once you realise this it allows you to let go of frus-tration and an-ger with others much quicker.
The person with the most flexibility will achieve the most.	If you don't get your result first time round, you keep doing some-thing different until you do. For example, the most adaptable person in your team is likely to be the one who finds the solution to a problem.	If you can stay flexible and open minded you will even-tually get the result that you want.
All behaviour has a positive intention behind it.	Why do people do what they do? For example, perhaps your member of staff who is off sick again has child-care issues. All behaviour starts with a positive intention by the person doing it. This does not	You may not agree with the behaviour, but if you look for the positive inten-tion behind it, it allows you to have more choice in how you respond and the solutions

(Continued)

Principle	What it means	So what?
	necessarily mean it will also benefit the person or people that the behaviour is 'done to'.	that you might find.
We control our minds and therefore our results.	You have choices about what you think and you know your thoughts influence your results. For example, you always have a choice about how you feel. You do not have to feel anxious about an appraisal meeting with your boss, you can choose to feel upbeat and positive.	Because results are dependent on your mental state, you want to be in the best state to achieve the outcomes you want. You can change your state by changing your thoughts.
We have all the resources we need to succeed.	People have the capacity to be, do and have whatever they want. For example, leaders should search out the potential of others in their team.	Most of us have largely untapped reserves of qualities, skills and attitudes that we have not yet learned to use.
The mind and body are interconnected.	There is a link between your thoughts and what you manifest in your body. For example, you don't get the best results when you feel bad about yourself or a situation.	You can influence your results by the way you think. That gives you control and choice over how you behave.

(*Continued*)

Principle	What it means	So what?
There is a solution to every problem.	Finding new solutions to old problems is at the heart of creativity. For example, it's much more motivational for your staff to work for a leader who seeks possibilities rather than problems.	This gives you confidence that you will always find a way to achieve what you want.
If something isn't working, do something different.	If you always do what you've always done, you always get what you've always got! For example, if you are resistant to change an outdated process or method you are missing out on the likelihood of an improved result.	If your strategy isn't working, ask yourself what you can do differently next time. Keep changing your approach until you find something that works.
Anything less than 100% is sabotage.	If you go for something in a half-hearted way you are stopping yourself from succeeding. For example, if you 'try' to be a good leader are you going to put your heart and soul into it?	Jedi master Yoda in Star Wars said: 'Do, or do not. There is no try.' If you decide to go for something then give it 100% and encourage your teams to do the same.

Imagine for a moment that you adopted these principles as a leader and you applied them with your staff. What difference would it make to you and to them? Many people talk about a 'positive' mindset yet they never explain what that is or how it can be achieved. These principles give you a positive mindset. They do this because they enable you to focus on learning and development as opposed to mistakes and criticism, being flexibile as opposed to being rigid, having choice as opposed to feeling stuck, dealing with situations quickly and moving on as opposed to dwelling on the negatives, feeling calmer about complex situations as opposed to feeling stressed, and having a laser beam focus on results as opposed to half-hearted efforts.

Your staff would feel supported and listened to as opposed to being 'difficult', developed as opposed to frustrated, able to make mistakes as opposed to being fearful, encouraged to have new ideas as opposed to being stuck, and willing to support you 100% as opposed to looking for an escape route. This is the recipe for a well-motivated workforce and world-class results.

A new managing director on an NLP journey

Neville UK is a family-owned business, supplying catering equipment and tableware to the professional catering sector. Nevilles, as they are known, has seen significant growth in the last two years through their focus on customer service, competitive product proposition and listening to customers. Andrew Neville recently became MD, and two weeks later embarked on his NLP Practitioner journey. Here are a few specific examples where he has embraced the principles of pre-suppositions of NLP:

● Massive lesson No. 1: Different models of the world. I learned that I was not as interested as I should be in other people's points of view. Now I really focus on listening as a leader to words, tonality and body language.

- Massive lesson No. 2: There is no failure, only feedback. Develop a culture where it's OK to make mistakes, make sure as a leader that you put yourself at the head of the list, it shows you're human!

- Massive lesson No. 3: The meaning of your communication is the response you get. Don't expect to always get the response that you want – your team will respond, often in non-verbal ways. Learn from the times you do not get the response you expected.

- Massive lesson No. 4: We have all of the resources we need to succeed. Create the working environment that allows you and your team to be able to access that state of creativity and innovation – hold your nerve and keep pushing for more creativity in others.

- Massive lesson No. 5: There is a solution to every problem. Re-frame problems into opportunities for solutions – for example, we had great feedback from our customer service questionnaire. However, we had one very poor feedback response from a customer. We spent some time talking to this customer to see how their experience had been poor, and identified a gap in our service offering. From this we were able to make a very simple change to our procedure, minimising drastically the risk of re-occurrence of the problem.

'NLP has helped me to develop my leadership style to help me access resourceful states in my staff. By respecting their model of the world I am able to empower them. For example, by giving goals and aims that provide guidelines that help, but do not stifle creativity, my teams can really develop their skills and be creative.' Andrew Neville, MD

Exercise 7: Living the principles

In NLP we often talk about 'Acting as If' something is true. That enables you to 'try' something on and see how it feels. It also starts to develop new neural connections and unconscious habits. In this exercise I want you to 'Act as If' all these twelve principles are true for you. Adopt them at work for one month and notice the difference, not only in the way that you behave as a result but also in the reaction of your staff to your new behaviours. You might even ask for feedback at the end of the month about the differences that your staff notice in you. Maybe they will notice you being calmer, less stressed, listening more, finding out about their strengths and encouraging them to experiment with new ideas.

Make a note below of how it felt to adopt these principles for one month:

What specific results did you get?

What feedback did you get from those around you?

Because of their background in cybernetics the pre-suppositions arguably give NLP a stronger theoretical foundation than is found in many other approaches to people development, including many forms of coaching. Though they are not claimed to be accurate statements about how the world 'really' is they encourage learning, responsibility, flexibility, focus, empowerment and choice. If you want to stand out from the crowd as a leader then these will help you to achieve just that.

Thinking differently

Here are some other core structures or frames of NLP that are generally believed to develop empowering ways of thinking and behaving even further. You will not find these in any book written by Bandler and Grinder, but they are taught by a wide range of NLP Institutes. These frames are:

- Cause vs Effect

- Responsibility for Results

- Perception is Projection

Which side are you on?

Consider for a moment. How do you behave as a leader? Do you generally look on the positive side of whatever happens at work or do you focus on the negatives and how to avoid taking the blame when things go wrong? I'm sure you've experienced a 'teflon' manager who appears to get away with things by ensuring that others take the blame. How about you? What is your starting point, your point of view? Some leaders will always see the opportunities in a situation whereas others will only see the problems. It depends on how you view it. Are you someone who takes responsibility for whatever happens to you or are you someone who blames others or circumstances for whatever happens? Does this sound familiar to you? For example, do you recognise yourself as someone who says, 'Yes, let's go for it', or are you the person who says, 'Yes, I'd like to but…'. Are you involved, interested and active in what you do, or are you buffeted by events, feeling out of control, disempowered, a victim?

In NLP this is called being either **at cause** or **at effect** of everything that goes on around you. Are you taking responsibility for what you create? It's a common thread in other self-help books. I do not believe that it's coincidental that you hear the same viewpoint over and over again. Successful leaders talk about being 'at cause' in one form or another although they may give it another title or name. This is not the way that most people behave. One of our finest skills as humans is to absolve ourselves of responsibility. When something goes well, we like to take credit for it; when something goes badly, we tend to shift blame. Once you put yourself 'at cause', and take responsibility, things will stop simply 'happening' to you, and you actively start to become the leader that you want to be.

Leading from 'effect'

'The British screwed us,' were Henry Paulson's words when he learned of the UK's Financial Services Authority's (FSA) decision not to approve a guarantee which would have allowed Barclays to buy Lehman.

This led to Paulson's contentious call to allow Lehman Brothers to fall, a decision which wiped hundreds of billions of pounds from global equities, and sent world stock markets into freefall. The former US Treasury Secretary's book, *On the Brink*, reveals how he blames the FSA for not helping the stricken bank. This is a great example of a leader on the 'effect' side of leadership. Rather than take responsibility for what Lawrence McDonald, a former Lehman trader, called a 'colossal failure of common sense' in his book of the same name, Paulson blames the FSA, who many still say were willing to do a deal if the US Treasury were prepared to share the risk.

I do not claim to be an expert in the Lehman affair; what I observe is the behaviour of the former Treasury Secretary to attempt to offload the blame for the collapse of the global financial markets which ensued.

A leader on the effect side sits around waiting for things to happen without taking responsibility for making anything happen themselves. They blame others when things do not go their way. They make excuses and find reasons why they cannot do what is required of them. It is disempowering, not only for them but also for their team members who know that their manager is not interested in improving the current situation. It's also no fun to be led by someone who is constantly moaning about their problems. These leaders 'at effect' give away their power because they always look to others to find the solution. They believe they have no alternatives. However, the reality is that they have chosen not to take any responsibility for their actions. The only advantage of focusing on excuses is that there is usually somebody else to blame! Often in large businesses, you come across experts at finding reasons why things haven't gone to plan. Sometimes there are entire committees of them.

In NLP it's often said that you get one of two things in life – the result you want or reasons why you didn't get the result. What I find a lot in business is the theory of collective responsibility or management by committee. It appears to me that the role of most committees is to find enough 'reasons' as to why one target or another has not been achieved. The irony is that if they find enough reasons for failing, those responsible still seem to walk away proudly patting themselves on the back. Is that how you want to behave? Maybe you even recognise some of that behaviour in yourself or you have colluded with that type of behaviour in the past.

Leading from 'cause'

'I don't believe in a little word like "can't".'

Richard Branson takes calculated risks. He is bold and takes responsibility for what happens in his business and personal adventures. He says: 'Some you win and some you lose. Be glad when you win. Don't have regrets when you lose. Never look back. You can't change the past. I try to learn from it.'

This is very much the spirit of those leaders who operate 'at cause'. They operate from a premise that on some level we create everything that happens in our lives. Now I don't know if we do create everything that happens to us, but accepting that we do puts us in a position of power over everything around us. More than anything else, this singular action will help you step up your game. That's because, whatever occurs in your life, good or bad, you are focused on what there is to learn from that situation. You feel much more in control of your life because you are taking responsibility. The result is that you keep your own personal power in any situation. Anyone moving from 'effect' to 'cause' feels empowered and stronger than they did before. Much of NLP is effectively designed to put us back 'at cause'. Those of us on the 'cause' side are always searching inside for a solution and to learn from our mistakes. This can sometimes seem like a tougher journey than the one experienced by those people 'at effect' – and yet it is one over which you keep complete control. Those 'at effect' keep their heads in the sand by blaming others for their own shortcomings. I prefer to keep control of my own destiny, no matter how tough the lessons can be at times. Leaders 'at cause' are decisive in creating what they want. If they are not getting the results they want, they learn from their experiences and move on to new possibilities. Above all, they believe they have choices in what they do and how they react to people and events.

If you want to move from the 'effect' to the 'cause' side of the equation, the first step is to remove all of your excuses. To do this, you must ask yourself the following questions when you don't get the results that you want:

● How have I managed to create this situation and for what purpose?

● What is there for me to learn from this?

● What do I need to do differently next time?

Soon you will notice that by asking yourself these questions you will start to get different results. Remember NLP pre-supposition No. 3: 'there is no failure only feedback'. Feedback is all about getting the learning from any situation. This way of thinking allows you to let things go and move on much more quickly than most of the population who often remain stuck in the past. When we talk about learnings they must come in a particular format for them to work.

Learnings are always:

● For you personally

● Positive

● For the future.

Fundamentally, learnings are for you because you cannot control someone else's behaviour. They are what you will do differently in future, not what you shouldn't or won't do again as this focuses your attention in the wrong direction. They are always for the future as the past has already happened. So after a tough meeting with your boss when you didn't get the raise you wanted, a learning might be:

'I will prepare much more thoroughly in future before I meet my boss, listing all the ways I'm valuable to this business.'

as opposed to

> 'My boss is an idiot who just doesn't get how valuable I am to this business.'

This is a very important distinction.

Exercise 8: Four steps to 'cause'

You now have an opportunity to operate 'at cause' for one month. You can do this at work and maybe even at home too. If you're not sure what to do at first, just pretend – act 'as if'. Enjoy the experience and reflect on what you're learning.

Step 1 Be 'at cause' at work. This means no more excuses! Take responsibility for everything that happens in your work life.

Step 2 Whatever happens to you, good or bad, ask yourself for what purpose did you create that situation and what there is for you to learn from it.

Step 3 Reflect on what you have learned from these situations. Do something different if you need to.

Step 4 Keep focusing on what you want to create in your work life. Go for it!

Responsibility for results

I often tell my clients that I am their 'tour guide'. I can assist them to make the changes that they need to make and I'll do whatever it takes to do that. However, in the end they have to take action, to do something differently or risk remaining in the Grey Zone. You are responsible for your own success. And when you begin to take 100 per cent responsibility for your life, amazing things begin to happen. What I've learned from my own experiences and those of my clients is as follows:

- When you take 100% responsibility for achieving your outcome and are willing to do it all by yourself, you won't have to.

- To the extent that you are not willing to do it all by yourself, you'll have to.

- When you don't take 100% responsibility for achieving your outcome you are not working magic, you are playing with luck.

- The only benefit of not taking 100% responsibility for achieving your outcome is that you'll always have someone to blame.

Perception is projection

Carl Jung, one of the founders of modern day psychology, said that everything we perceive outside is a projection from inside. We can't perceive anything that is not in some way an example of us. All our work and personal relationships help us to find out things about ourselves. Situations are not real, they are only our projections of what we believe is going on. For example, you can de-brief an important meeting with a work colleague and end up wondering if you were even at the same meeting. That is because you both have a very different experience of the meeting as you have each filtered the experience differently.

Mihaly Csikszentmihalyi is one of the few people to have analysed the processing power of the brain. He estimates that our nervous system – through our five senses of sight, sound, taste, smell and touch – is bombarded by two million bits of data each second of the day. We can only digest approximately 126 bits of that data – or between five and nine manageable chunks each second. We filter out the rest of the data by deleting, distorting and generalising information that we 'don't need'. That's a lot of data to get rid of. No wonder two people remember the same event differently, as the 126 bits of data that you focus on will be different from the 126 bits of data that I focus on. It's as if each of us has a giant sieve in our nervous system and the 126 holes in my sieve are different from yours. Some may overlap and others will be very different. Therefore, when my two million bits of information are sieved through, I focus on different information and have a completely different experience to you. The 126 bits of data then create what in NLP we call our 'internal representations' or, in other words, our thoughts.

What we delete, distort and generalise depends upon the values and beliefs we have accumulated over the years. Because we all filter the events through our different value and belief systems, our filters act like a pair of sunglasses, letting through only those things which we decide unconsciously to pay attention to. For example, if I have low self-esteem and I believe I'm not good enough, I will filter out all the times I've been successful and only notice the times I haven't. The good news is that if you change your filters it will change your perception and your experience of a situation.

For example, let's assume you have a difficult and tense relationship with your boss. If you are at cause, you acknowledge that you have created that relationship. If you ask yourself how you'd like to behave differently in that situation you would begin to change how you view and feel about that person. The result would be that your experience of them will change. Experiment with this and notice your results. I guarantee you'll be amazed.

In addition, your staff will not actualise anything you do not believe to be possible or true. If you view your staff as resourceful and magnificent, they will perform at a higher level than if you believe they are useless. This is because what you believe to be true is projected out to those around you through your behaviours and your language. A report into self-actualisation and teachers (Clark and Steuart, 1990) concluded that:

> 'The way we view the world will always be in direct accordance to how we view ourselves. When we are sad, we see a hopeless place. When we are afraid, we see everyone as a threat. When we are whole, we see a common future...Self-actualizing persons see the possibilities for themselves and for others. They become leaders because they are treading a path upon which we are all headed.'

This is an important feature of the 'Winning State of Mind' because we learn that we can change our current model of the world as a leader and the way that we view those in it. We do this by changing our own beliefs or filters. None of us experience the 'real' world. Alfred Korzybski, who came to the attention of Bandler and Grinder in the early 1970s, developed the central idea of 'the map is not the territory'. The territory is the 'real' world. Our own personal maps are our interpretation of the territory; they are not true but generalised, deleted and distorted. Because of this our maps can be changed and I'll show you how in the next section.

The NLP communication model

Our thoughts start a chain reaction in our nervous system that is important for leaders to understand and explore. The information that you unconsciously filter into your nervous system via all your senses forms your thoughts or, in NLP-speak, your internal representations. Your thoughts are made up of a combination of your senses, i.e. pictures, sounds, feelings, tastes and smells. Everyone has a sensory preference in terms of how they view the world. What do you believe your preference to be? For example, if you see pictures as you think, you probably have a visual preference. If you have strong feelings as you think, you probably have a kinaesthetic or feelings preference, and so on. You'll find out your exact preference in Chapter 10, 'Influencing with Integrity'.

What's important is that the type of thoughts you have will drive how you feel – or your emotional state. If you think back to a time when you were very successful, I'm sure it occurred when you were in a very positive emotional state or mood. You are unlikely to have been depressed, miserable or anxious. So our results are dependent on our mood or state.

What happens next is that our mental state drives our physiology or body language, our physiology drives our behaviour, and our behaviour ultimately drives our results. So it follows that our thoughts will drive our results – hence, thoughts become things. As Henry Ford said: 'Think you can, think you can't; either way, you'll be right.'

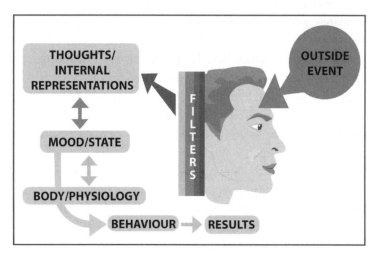

NLP Communication Model

Let's explore an example of this chain reaction. Imagine you need to have a challenging conversation with a member of your team. That is the external event that triggers the chain reaction. If you have had a number of unsuccessful conversations with that person in the past, you are likely to be filtering that imminent conversation in a negative way. That is to say, you expect the conversation to go badly so, in your head, you begin to tell yourself a story about the conversation going badly. Your thoughts are then focused on the conversation going badly. In turn, that will affect how you feel – and your mood or state. You are likely to feel nervous, uncomfortable, and any other variety of negative emotions. And because the mind and body are interconnected, this then impacts your physiology. When you go to have the conversation, the 'receiver' will notice your nervousness. For example, they might spot you fidgeting. Your behaviour is then compromised because you are nervous, and the other person picks up your anxiety and plays on it. The final outcome is that you did not get the result that you wanted. Hence, a self-fulfilling prophecy.

The opposite is also true. Let's take the same situation. You have a challenging conversation coming up. This time you remind yourself of the times when you have had successful conversations with this person, which have led to a great result. This time you are looking forward to the meeting, as you are very confident of your success. You tell yourself a success story and maybe even imagine how you will be feeling at the end of the successful conversation. You are feeling confident and full of anticipation. This time your physiology is different – your posture is much more positive (i.e. you are standing tall, grounded, open and smiling). Your 'receiver' notices how positive you are feeling and responds. You are able to get your point of view across successfully and make some new agreements. You get the result you wanted.

The same external situation has completely different outcomes, each of which is entirely dependent upon how you filtered the event from inside of you. The next exercise is designed to bring to your conscious attention the type of thoughts that you have.

//

Exercise 9: What are you thinking about?

Take a few moments now to let your mind relax a little. Just as you can be aware of the feelings and movements in your body, you can also step back from your thoughts and simply observe them. One thought drifts in which leads to another and then another until you become lost in your own world. What I want you to do is to observe your thoughts as they come and go. Just sit still and wait for a thought to arise without attaching any meaning to it. Simply observe them coming and going. Do this initially for about five minutes.

Over the next day, pay attention to your thoughts and feelings. Notice if your thoughts are positive and empowering, or do you beat yourself up a lot of the time? Do you focus on what you've done well or on your mistakes? Make a note of the recurring patterns below, both positive and negative. You may be surprised by the results. Which side of the scales is the heaviest? If it's your negative thoughts, then you have a huge opportunity right now to start changing your thoughts from the inside out.

Positive thoughts and feelings	Negative thoughts and feelings

How do I change my thoughts?

There are many ways to change our thoughts. One key way is to change what you believe about yourself, thereby changing your filters. What do I mean by beliefs? Our beliefs are views or ideas we have about ourselves, other people and situations that we hold to be true. Our beliefs are mainly formed before we reach the age of seven. We collect beliefs from those closest to us at that time, such as parents, teachers, church leaders, close family, and any other significant people in our lives. The most important thing to understand about beliefs is that they are generalisations that we create from life experiences. Most of us do not consciously decide what we believe. Furthermore, once we have a belief we forget that it can be changed, and it becomes our reality. Now that's scary. We rarely challenge our long-held beliefs and they become a filter through which we sieve all of our life's expectations and experiences. So, if I don't believe I'm good enough, then I filter all my experiences through that belief until I only notice the times this is true. I don't notice all the times I was successful, or even *more* than good enough. What do you think about this? Does this resonate with you at all?

Sometimes one careless comment from a person who is influential in your life can shape what you (unconsciously) decide is possible for the rest of your life. For example, if a parent tells their child that they are stupid, it can have a lifelong impact. What they didn't know at the time was that even a throwaway and seemingly 'harmless' comment can do untold damage. I'm sure that if parents realised this they would be so much more careful about what they say to their children. The important thing is that once we learn how beliefs are formed, we have the opportunity to change them and break the negative patterns of our past. I wonder how your belief system has influenced and impacted upon your successes until now?

You can take steps to change your beliefs and I'm going to show you how to do this. First you'll note both the limiting and empowering beliefs you've become aware of about yourself.

If you're not sure how to get started, think about the areas at work where you are not yet getting the results you want. Are you in the leadership role you know you are capable of achieving? If not, why not? It's likely that there are limiting beliefs which are holding you back. What do you think they are? What are the recurring patterns you've noticed so far? The next exercise will help you find out.

Exercise 10: My beliefs

Step 1: My limiting beliefs

Examples of limiting beliefs include:

- Negations – e.g. I'm not capable, I can't get the results I want, I'm too old
- Comparatives – e.g. I'm not good enough
- Generalisations – e.g. I always fail at interview panels
- All beliefs – e.g. I don't believe I can do it

Now, brainstorm all your limiting beliefs about yourself and write them down below:

Step 2: My empowering beliefs

Examples of empowering beliefs include:

- I'm good at what I do
- My staff like me
- I'm a confident person

Next, consider areas at work where you are getting the results you want. What empowering beliefs are helping you to achieve them? For example, if you've been promoted quickly, maybe that's because you are viewed as a 'can-do' character and able to deliver results. You get the idea. Don't worry if what you write is not quite spot on; just brainstorm with yourself for now and write down your empowering beliefs below:

Step 3: My three most empowering beliefs

Choose your three most empowering beliefs and, for a week, keep a record below of all those occasions when those specific beliefs have enabled you to get your desired result. For example, if you circled the belief 'I can motivate my team', observe the times when you have done this. Notice how good that felt and how often you did it. I bet your empowering beliefs are more active in your life than you realised.

Step 4: My three most limiting beliefs

Next, circle your three most limiting beliefs and ask yourself the cost of failing to let go of these beliefs, in terms of your goals. In other words, if you don't let them go, how will your goals be compromised? Write down the answers below and be honest with yourself.

That wasn't pleasant was it? It wasn't meant to be. If you associate enough pain with a situation it often provides the 'tipping point', or impetus, for change. You may find that your limiting beliefs have already begun to be shaken up just by being aware of them and recognising the negative impact they have on your life.

Step 5: Changing your limiting beliefs

Work with each of your limiting beliefs in turn.

Take your first limiting belief – e.g. 'I'll never get the promotion I deserve'. As you think about that belief, notice the image that comes into your mind. Notice what you see, hear and feel. Play around with the image by dimming the brightness of the picture, moving it further away from you, turning down the volume of any sounds and making any feelings less intense. Sounds weird, I know, but our brains can do this easily!

Then ask yourself: What's the opposite of that limiting belief? In this case it is 'I will get the promotion I deserve'. As you think about getting that promotion, notice the image that comes into your mind. Notice what you see, hear and feel. This time, really ramp up all your senses, especially your feelings. Make the picture brighter, the sounds louder and the feelings stronger. You'll know you're doing this right when you start to feel great about this idea. Now you are ready to start.

1. Get back the image that you will never get the promotion you deserve. Now, replace it with the image that you *will* get the promotion that you deserve. Make this image even more compelling each time you access it. Do it fast and really go for it!

2. Continue doing this until you can no longer access the first image – all you have clearly in your mind is the new empowering image of you in that amazing new position.

At first, you may find that you can get the idea of the limiting belief very easily, and the idea of the opposite or more positive idea may take longer. That's fine. As you turn up the brightness, sounds and feelings, the intensity will change. Even if you can only get the opposite or positive ideal briefly at first, it is fine. You will notice that it becomes easier as the old limiting belief fades away. Once the old belief starts to fade away you know you are close to being finished. Keep going until it disappears completely.

Now ask yourself how you feel about that old limiting belief. Do the same for your other limiting beliefs and notice them freeing up and moving out of your system.

Keep focusing on your new empowering beliefs and you will be surprised how you begin to experience the world in a more positive and empowered way.

Doing whatever it takes

Peter is a coaching client of mine. He's a transport manager for a global distribution company. When he was promoted into a middle manager role he was required to make a short presentation each week to the senior managers in his Division about the potential problems in the week ahead. He had a real fear of presenting and at the first meeting collapsed and was taken away to hospital in an ambulance. So this was a severe case. His Director asked me to get involved and Peter worked through the limiting beliefs he had about himself. He was doing quite a number on himself, focusing on all the awful things that would happen to him when he messed up. He traced this pattern of behaviour back to his early childhood when his father had emotionally abused him whenever he didn't perform in the way expected of him. He worked on identifying his limiting beliefs about himself. He was surprised that at some of them had been held at an unconscious level for over 30 years. I worked with him to begin to change these beliefs and to show him that they were only generalisations and not really true. I also gave him some strategies for managing his feelings in those situations when he had to present. Although he'll never volunteer to present at the O2 arena, Peter is now managing the weekly meeting without any challenges.

The work we did together really brought into perspective the huge impact of our limiting beliefs – not only can they hold us back, but they can also impact on our health. However, the good news is that once they are brought into our conscious awareness we can begin to change them and recognise how ridiculous they actually are. We can create our future and creating new empowering beliefs is taking the first step forwards. Imagine what impact changing your limiting beliefs will have on your filters and consequently your mind-set and results in business and in your life.

Focus on what you want

The last piece in terms of building a 'Winning State of Mind' is to focus on what you want to achieve. Why is this important to us as leaders? Firstly, the brain cannot process negatives; when we are told: 'Don't think of a blue elephant', a blue elephant is exactly what we think of. In that moment we focus on the very thing we don't want, making our nervous system very aware of it. So it's vital that you focus on what you want, not what you don't want. Go back and make sure that your personal leadership goals are about what you want to achieve, and are not negative in any way. No one would ever deliberately attract what they don't want into their lives. It simply comes from a lack of awareness. This also important in the wider context of our roles as leaders. Do you communicate by telling your staff what you don't want them to do and then are disappointed by the results? Be clear about what you want them to do differently and then you'll get the results that you need.

Our secret weapon

When you focus on something – no matter what it happens to be – you are calling it into existence. It becomes a *self-fulfilling prophecy*. We already know that our vision and goals give us a target to aim for. What many of us may not know is that we have a part of our brain called the 'reticular activating system', or RAS for short. Your RAS plays a vital part in your ability to achieve goals because it acts like a laser beam, focusing on and bringing to your attention people, places and things that can help you get there. Your RAS is the automatic mechanism inside your brain that brings relevant information to your attention. It works as a filter between your conscious and your unconscious mind. It takes instructions from your conscious mind and passes them on to your unconscious. It's rather like an instruction from your conscious mind to your unconscious mind telling it to 'Focus on this...'. It's your RAS that does the work by paying attention to the thoughts lodged in your unconscious mind. You no longer have to re-visit those thoughts in an active conscious way. You will have done enough by setting clear goals to begin to attract the people, places and things to you that will help you achieve them. That's why your conscious mind is often called the 'Goal-Setter' and your unconscious the 'Goal-Getter'.

It's worth bearing in mind some interesting points about your RAS that make it an essential tool for achieving goals. Firstly, you can deliberately programme this system by choosing the exact messages you send from your conscious mind. You can do this by focusing on your personal leadership vision and goals. Secondly, your RAS cannot distinguish between 'real' events and 'imagined' reality. In other words, imagine yourself already having achieved your vision and goals. This 'visualisation' will improve your ability to attract in what you want to achieve. Athletes use this technique a lot – effectively rehearsing their sport in their mind before they actually go out and do it. When you set your goal you create a very definite image of it in your conscious mind. Your RAS will then pass this on to your unconscious mind – which will help you to achieve the goal. It does this by bringing to your attention all the relevant information which otherwise you might not have even noticed.

You have a choice right now. Do you want to believe that things just 'happen' and what happens to you is just the luck of the draw? Or do you want to believe and know that your future success as a leader is in your own hands and that your vision and goals will come into your life because of the way you think and what you focus on?

If you have no goals in life, then your RAS has nothing to go for. If you are drifting from one thing to the next with no focus, then your RAS does not have any clear instructions as to what it should seek out for you. I'm sure you know people who lead chaotic lives, not settling to anything for very long. Maybe you have experienced life like that up until this moment. Now there are no more excuses. Get your RAS working for you, and use the 126 bits of information you gather every second of your life to help you get what you want.

Giving our global leaders of tomorrow an edge

I was asked by Durham Business School to run a workshop for their MBA students. The workshop was called 'What Really makes the Difference – The Mindset and Attitudes of Successful Leaders using NLP' and covered the following four key themes:

1. *Where are you now?* This session covered a definition of NLP for business, the concept of The Business Grid and the importance of goal-setting. The students developed their own goals for the next year and worked together using the 'Keys to an achievable outcome' questions to ensure their goals will happen.

2. *Focus on what you want.* Here I covered the NLP communications model and the chain reaction that comes

from the link between our thoughts, feelings, physiology and behaviour. I also included the importance of focusing on what you want rather than what you don't want. The students had fun discovering their own communication styles (see Chapter 10) and developed their flexibility around communication.

3. *Results vs Reasons.* One of my favourite sessions which challenged whether the delegates were at cause or effect in their lives. We also covered the other key NLP frames and responsibility for results. The students experienced what it's like to live at cause and the potential difference to them as leaders.

4. *Believe you can.* A very stimulating session that got the students to examine the pre-suppositions of NLP and to identify how they will use them to change their model of the world. We then considered their limiting and empowering beliefs about themselves and they practiced changing a limiting belief.

The workshop finished with a powerful action metaphor that challenged the delegates' beliefs about what is possible for them. Dr Julie Hodges, Director of FT MBA Programme and Senior Teaching Fellow at Durham Business School said:

'As part of the skills development programme for students we were keen to run a creative and innovative session to enhance the students' communication skills, rapport building and goal setting capabilities. The NLP session focused on skills applicable to the business world and enabled the students to improve their presentation skills. The NLP principles and skills underlie much of what is taught in negotiation seminars. Many of the students have said that they learned skills which will help them during the rest of their MBA and in their future careers.'

Pulling it all together

Let's reflect back on what makes the 'Winning State of Mind' and what could happen to your results if you were to adopt these features. As a reminder here are the core elements:

1. Embrace the twelve core principles of NLP. This means taking them on as your own beliefs about the world and using them not only on yourself but also with those around you. For example, notice how respecting other models of the world helps you become more flexible and how your communication improves once you take on board that it is only successful if you get the results that you want.

2. Live life on the cause side of the equation and take responsibility for everything that happens to you. Whether we do create everything in our world or not, this model gives us an empowering way to experience the world and to learn and improve when things don't go to plan.

3. Taking 100% responsibility for the results that you want will mean that you keep going until you get the results that you want. Those around you will be willing to support you as they experience your 100% commitment to the job in hand. So when you are willing to take 100% responsibility you'll often find that you won't have to.

4. Bring your thoughts and beliefs into conscious awareness so you can change them. Understand that you perceive the world through your filters and that these can be changed once you know what they are. Rebalance the level of positivity in your thoughts to give you the best chance of achieving your goals.

5. Change your limiting beliefs about yourself so you start to filter the world through far more positive experiences. Notice how this changes everything and especially your potential and your results.

6. Finally, focus on what you want to achieve so your RAS can put to work the 126 bits of data that you receive each second of your life. Move to a position of strength so you draw to yourself those people, places and things that will support you in achieving your personal leadership vision and goals.

Exercise 11: Let's get started

Imagine yourself in a year's time having embraced all these elements of the 'Winning State of Mind'. Look back to now:

- How would your behaviour be different to now?
- What would you be focused on?
- What would you have achieved?

Write your answers below and use them to inspire you every day to think differently now.

Notice how your winning state of mind changes not only your effectiveness as a leader but improves other areas of your life as well.

3
MODELLING WORLD-
CLASS PERFORMANCE

//

I f someone can do it, anyone can do it. This is the basis of one
of the fundamental elements of NLP – modelling. Grinder
describes NLP as a modelling technology that generates a set
of differences between geniuses and average performers. I once
heard him say that modelling was the most revolutionary part
of NLP. The outcome of modelling is to produce a set of code
transferable to others. Every NLP technique or pattern has been
created by modelling. For example, the technique of rapport
(see Chapter 10) came from hypnosis when Bandler and Grinder modelled Milton Erickson. The idea of matching breathing
came from Conrad Lightman, another hypnotist. NLP does not
invent this code, rather it identifies the patterns in geniuses,
strips them down to a number of component parts, repackages
them and then makes them available to others. Modelling is
the methodology by which NLP came into being and the reason
why it plays such an important role in NLP. For example, the
Milton model was modelled from Milton Erickson and the Meta
Model from Virginia Satir, both world-class therapists.

This chapter explores the advantages of modelling and how to
model, and reviews the results from a number of recent modelling projects.

Why model?

In business there are many potential uses of modelling. Here are just a few:

- The ability to sell

- The capacity to manage any situation

- The ability to run a successful meeting/project/change programme, etc

- The confidence to deliver a compelling presentation

- The tactics to achieve a successful negotiation

- The charisma to lead a world-class business

There are many more. For example, Charles Faulkner, an NLP trainer and author, modelled the intuitive judgements of world-class financial traders and used the results to become a successful trader himself.

The key advantages of modelling are as follows:

- Fast-track the learning process (as a rule of thumb you can replicate any behaviour, ability or skill in half the time it took to teach the skill originally)

- Install the model in yourself

- Train trainers

- Roll-out training programmes to wider audiences

- Develop a high potential business

The NLP approach to modelling

Each of us has a particular set of strategies which enables us to function effectively in an organisation. These repetitive sequences of internal and external behaviour include strategies for delegating, for learning and teaching, for motivation, creativity, decision making and a thousand other functions. Yet these skills are most often acquired by unconscious trial and error and, because they are not obtained explicitly, we have little idea of how to transfer them to others.

What is more, people may succeed magnificently using one particular strategy for a certain function (defining company policy, for example), while seriously underachieving when they attempt to apply the same strategy elsewhere (for example, explaining those policies).

People use widely different internal processing strategies, and this accounts for the gap between mediocre and top performers. When you ask people who are really excellent, 'How do you do it?' the most common response is 'I don't really know' or 'I just...sort of...do it and everything happens naturally'. This is typical of 'unconscious competence'. By the end of the modelling project the person being modelled invariably says, 'Well, I never realised that's what I do,' and often they will add, 'I thought everyone did it that way!'

Until NLP, most approaches to modelling concentrated on studying external behaviour.

External behaviour is the conscious component of the activity that is easiest to observe and model because it's happening on the outside. However, if the most important distinctions are internal (i.e. values and beliefs and the strategies they adopt), traditional methods of modelling are of limited value.

Internal process and state are the unconscious components which were rarely included in a 'model' before NLP. In other words, NLP found ways of making conscious the out-of-awareness behaviours, mental habits and beliefs of top performers, as well as defining a code for describing these processes and teaching them to someone else.

Most people today accept that their ability to produce results effectively is influenced by their feelings, way of thinking, beliefs, values and sense of identity. It therefore becomes crucial to identify thinking strategies and other 'intangibles' that are so important in excellent managers, planners, trainers, sales representatives, and so on. In order to accurately define what their subjects were doing, Bandler, Grinder and others developed a new approach to modelling which encompassed both conscious and unconscious components:

- *External behaviour or what people do on the outside*: paying attention to physiology including breathing and posture (very important in modelling sports people)

- *Internal process or the strategy that people run*: this drives the external behaviour and it's formed of the sequence of events that make up the activity

- *Internal emotional state or what that person believes about the activity and how important it is to them*: this is the neglected area of modelling and it provides the reason why someone does something

Process not content

The general principles and methods of modelling are independent of the skill-set being modelled or the environment in which the modelling takes place. This is because modelling is based upon the process being adopted and not the content. Bandler and Grinder talked about behaviour being rule-governed. Grinder actually said that 'Patterns of excellence in human behaviour are rule-governed.'

So the question to ask is, 'What set of rules would account for the behaviour that we are observing?' In which case, the approach can be applied to almost any circumstance and is already being used extensively in business, education, health, sports, personal development and other application areas. In addition, NLP starts from the idea that all people are equal in terms of physical and mental capabilities. The only differences are the issues of motivation – values, beliefs, attitudes which drive someone to be excellent.

Stages of a modelling project

Preparation

Identify the skill that you want to model. For the purposes of this leadership section, consider a leadership style that you'd like to be able to replicate in yourself. For example, you may wish to model a leader who:

- Is able to build excellent rapport

- Achieves the best results in the organisation

- Can get and hold the audience's attention when presenting

- Can build a motivational vision that their staff feel compelled to follow

- Can give excellent feedback to their staff

- Can deal with a range of complex issues simultaneously

- Is very creative

Whatever the skill, choose something that would be of great value to you in your own development as a leader. Select a person or people who demonstrate the skill that you want to model at an excellent, even world-class, level. Make sure that you know what you mean by excellence. It's often helpful to define excellence in terms of the measurable results that your model of excellence achieves. In NLP terms, define excellence in terms of what you see, hear and feel when this top performer is displaying their skill. Here are a few things to consider:

- You may model different skills from different leaders. For example, whilst one might be a world-class presenter, another might be an excellent chair of meetings.

- Modelling involves separating out what is essential through to idiosyncratic. That means there will be activities or beliefs that do not contribute to the model yet they are done anyway. For example, an athlete might have a ritual that they perform before they take their turn, but this may not be essential to their strategy. We only discover these things by consciously starting to drop pieces to find what's essential.

- You may have to chunk a large behaviour down into its individual functions. For example, modelling 'leadership' is too big a chunk. Which specific part do you want to model?

- You do not physically have to interview your model if that is not possible. For example, if you want to model a world-class leader like Richard Branson you can read their books and watch them on TV and DVD, etc. This is not as good as a face-to-face study but it can still be done.

Modelling exercise

Assuming you are undertaking a face-to-face exercise, you need to agree a time or series of times when you can meet your modelling subject. It's important to build some leeway into your plans in case you have to go back to check out certain steps. Do your best to 'switch off' any of your own values, beliefs and experiences as you go through this process. It's important to clear your mind of your usual assumptions and judgements about the world. Think of it as getting out of your own way! Take a disassociated role to get the very best results. If you don't do this you may find yourself questioning the answers that you get from your modelling subject. Beware, as this is a tip-off that your own value judgements are getting in the way.

Step 1 - Observe your model in action to identify the following:

(a) Notice how they use their physiology. This is of course very important if you are modelling a sportsperson. However, in any activity, physiology can play a key role. According to Albert Mehrabian in *Silent Messages* it accounts for 55% of the impact of our communication. For example, if you are modelling presentation skills, how does your modelling subject hold themselves? Do they use many gestures? Do they use a lot of 'show and tell'? What other non-verbal behaviours do they utilise? Grinder said that non-verbal behaviour was far more important than any of the other components of modelling.

(b) Then notice how your model uses their language - both in the words they use and their tonality. Mehrabian said that words account for 7% of the impact of communications and tonality 38%. So it's not so much what we say but rather how we say it. Do they put a particular emphasis on specific words and how do they use their voice tonality? Do they use pauses in certain places or lower their tonality? What do you notice about their breathing? Do they repeat certain language patterns or phrases?

(c) What do they communicate about their values and beliefs? What model of the world do they operate from? This is about what they believe and what's important to them. For example, Richard Branson's book *Screw It, Let's Do It* is full of his beliefs. On the very first page he summarises his beliefs about his success: 'Believe it can be done, have goals, live life to the full, never give up, prepare well, have faith in yourself, help each other'. That tells us a huge amount about his model of the world that we can then begin to replicate.

Step 2 - Question your model

First of all get your model to imagine they are using or doing the skill you are modelling. In NLP we call this 'associating' into the activity. That really connects them into the process. Ask your questions in the present tense to help keep them associated. Then take them through each of the three core component areas that we discussed earlier. You want to find out about the 'what' and the 'how' rather than the 'why'.

External behaviour

It's often easier to start with the conscious part of their strategy. That means their external behaviour or what they do on the outside that you can observe.

Ask them 'what are you saying and doing'. Then compare this to what you actually observed. Check out any elements you observed that they didn't mention. These could be unconscious and/or idiosyncratic steps. Ask them to take you through how they use their posture and breathing. An excellent question to check out idiosyncratic steps is 'would it still work if you didn't do "x"'.

Internal process

Then take them step by step through what they do. This will draw out the sequence of events or the strategy that makes up the activity.

Ask them 'what's the very first thing that has to happen', then 'what's the next thing' and so on. Run them through the strategy many times until you have the core components. Again, strip out the idiosyncratic steps.

Internal emotional state

Finally, explore their internal emotional state which is likely to be the most unconscious part of their activity.

Ask them questions like 'what's important to you at this time or about this activity?' to elicit their values. Then ask, 'what do you believe about yourself/about others/about the situation in relation to this activity?' Make sure you understand their model of the world by trying it on yourself to see if it makes sense.

Step 3 – Conduct a sensitivity analysis

This will determine what's critical in order to get the same result as the model. Start changing things to find out if they make any difference. This will also help to strip out the idiosyncratic steps. Find out if stripping out any steps makes a difference in terms of results. If it makes a positive difference, keep the step in. If it makes no difference, strip it out. The real art of modelling is to simplify the model to its minimum components whilst still maintaining the results.

Step 4 – Install in yourself

This is the stage when you replicate the model that you have elicited. Do you get the same results as the experts? If you do, great. If not, go back and check you have all the crucial components in the right order. Keep practising until you replicate your model's results completely.

Step 5 – Universal training design

Once you have mastered the model perfectly, you can go on to teach it to others. Select a group of 'normal' performers and set a benchmark of their current results. Then teach them the model and measure by how much their results improve. The model can then be refined and documented.

You can also use the model to produce a profile of a typical top performer to be used as part of the organisation's recruitment and selection process (and train the recruiters to recruit against it).

Summary

Allow enough time with each of the top performers in the context within which they use their skills as well as follow-up interviews. Similarly, some average performers will need to be studied in the same context for comparison. This approach to modelling offers a proven method for discovering what top performers do that makes them so effective. Once this has been achieved other members of the organisation can learn to replicate the effective behaviour and strategies to improve their own performance.

Story – The shrinking joint of beef

A newly married couple were cooking Sunday roast for the family for the very first time. The husband was curious as he watched his new wife chop off the end of a succulent beef joint before it was wrapped, put into the roasting tin and cooked. When he asked her about this she said that her mother had always cooked a perfect joint of beef in this way. As her mother was coming for lunch she suggested her new husband ask her why she cut off the end of the beef joint before cooking. When his new mother-in-law arrived he duly asked her the question. She looked surprised and said that her mother had always done that and cooked a perfect joint of beef in this way. As her mother was also coming for lunch she suggested he speak to his grandmother-in-law about why she cut off the end of the beef joint before cooking. When grandmother arrived he duly asked her the question. She looked surprised as she told him that it was the only way the joint of beef would fit into her roasting tin!

Exercise 12: Undertake a modelling project in the context of leadership

Following the step-by-step approach above conduct your own modelling project. Ask yourself what skills would be most useful for you to develop in your leadership role. Then pick a modelling subject and get started. It's easiest if this model is already in your business but you may have to go further afield to find a world-class example. In my experience, if you tell someone you admire them and would like to learn from them they are unlikely to turn you away. Write the results of your project below and consider how best you can leverage these valuable lessons more widely in your business. Maybe it would add value to train many others in the same process.

Step 1 – Observe your model in action

Step 2 - Question your model

1 External behaviour:

2 Internal process:

3 Internal state:

Step 3 - Conduct a sensitivity analysis

Key learning points:

Step 4 - Install in yourself

Key learning points:

Step 5 – Other applications in my business

Summary

1 What was the most important learning for you?

2 By how much have your results improved since adopting the model?

3 How much time did you save yourself as a result of your modelling project?

Modelling for personal transformation

What follows are the stories of two of my students, set a modelling project as part of their NLP Master Practitioner programme.

Marie – learning to do whatever it takes

Marie is the owner of a small training business that delivers training to contact centre staff. She chose the owner of a corporate training company as her modelling subject because they were in a similar business to her own and Marie wanted some tips to help her business survive a tough recession.

She conducted her modelling study through a series of face-to-face interviews. She found an iterative process worked well. This involved her gathering data, then reviewing it and checking for what else was required.

Out of the three core modelling areas, Marie discovered that 'Internal Emotional State' held the most important information for her as her modelling subject held very different beliefs and values to her own. This was very exciting for her. Most importantly, Marie learned that her subject had had a rock solid belief in herself from an early age – unlike Marie, who had struggled with her self-image for many years. Her subject had always been prepared to 'do whatever it takes' to grow her business (as long as it was in line with her beliefs and values). She had also created multiple income streams to help protect her business in challenging times. She was also clear about being flexible – if something in her strategy wasn't working then she would quickly adapt and Marie realised she needed to be more open to change if she was to succeed in the same way.

The result was that Marie modelled her subject's key beliefs and values, especially to 'do whatever it takes' to keep the business alive and to 'remain flexible' on the journey. Marie realised that she had all her eggs in one basket. Her business had a single revenue stream and all the risk was in one place. Previously, she had also declined any associate work as it hadn't felt right to represent another company's brand. As a result, she had turned away valuable revenue opportunities for her business. Marie began to diversify and to collaborate with other training companies, offering her services as a freelance consultant wherever possible and soon her business and cash-flow were firmly back on track.

Katie – Using modelling to improve HR practice

Katie is an HR manager working in a pharmaceuticals business. She chose a female ex-Chief Executive of a Borough Council who now holds a major role in the Arts Council. The objective for Katie was to discover her model's strategies for achieving success. The modelling exercise was conducted over two meetings – one over the phone whilst her model was in the House of Commons in London. Again, the key distinctions were in the area of 'Internal Emotional State'. Katie learned that her subject's ethos was not necessarily to be the best, but to be the best she could be. Her strong belief that people are inherently good means that she generally expects and receives reciprocal support and achievement. She is also very focused and never loses sight of the overall goal.

Katie has modelled these beliefs by changing her approach, delegating more to others, focusing on building strong relationships and enabling others to shine. This allows her to stay focused on the overall outcome, making for better working relationships and ultimately greater chance of success.

By way of a specific example, Katie works in a small team of five HR practitioners. In April 2009 the HR Director left and a replacement was appointed. At around the same time, two colleagues also left the business. With 60% of the team new, it was crucial that the new members were given strong support and guidance in order that they could very quickly become effective in role. Katie worked hard to understand the strengths of her new colleagues and build strong relationships such that they were able to become operationally effective. This was recognised by the business and resulted in a pay rise and an exceptional bonus payment in August 2009.

These two case studies show how modelling can be applied in the 'real' world with great results. Marie took some focused action to save her business and Katie adapted her leadership style in a way that was recognised by her organisation with a promotion and a bonus payment. Both examples found the key distinctions in the 'internal state' component of the model. Marie and Katie found that what their subjects believed about themselves and what was important to them about their leadership style gave them their greatest insights. In another modelling project, external behaviour or internal process could be equally important.

The key element of modelling is to bring a skill to the level of conscious competence so it can be taught to others. Once you understand the process you can adopt modelling as a critical leadership strategy. It is a way of generating excellence in everything you do as a leader, as a team and as a business. Modelling is a powerful technique because it works and, as the case studies show, it really makes a difference.

Pulling it all together

Let's reflect on the leadership journey you've taken in the first part of this book and pull together the main facets of your own leadership model.

In Chapter 1, 'Building Strategies for Success', you developed your Personal Leadership Vision and your Personal Leadership Goals. In Chapter 2, 'A Winning State of Mind', you shifted your leadership to the 'cause' side of the spectrum and began to take responsibility for creating what you want as well as changing those limiting beliefs about your potential that had been holding you back. In Chapter 3, you modelled a world-class example or examples of leadership to fast-track your own development. Now let's pull this altogether in your own model of leadership for the future. What kind of leader do you want to be so others ask to model you?

We are going to develop your model by using the three core components of modelling: external behaviour, internal process and internal state.

Exercise 13: What's my leadership model?

Step 1: External behaviour

What is it that people are going to notice about you? For example:

- How will you dress?
- How will you sound?
- How will you use your physiology? For example, do you want to come across as a grounded leader? A leader with gravitas? Or do you want to be a powerful presence in the background?

- How are you going to behave with your team? For example, is humour going to be a focus of your style?
- Are you going to be a visible leader and be out amongst your team or will you operate from your ivory tower?
- What's most important to you?

Step 2: Internal process

How will you lead your team?

- What's your step by step strategy for leadership? For example: What's your step-by-step approach to a normal day?
- How do you communicate with your staff?
- What's your leadership style? For example, will you be a directive or a collaborative leader or will you be flexible depending upon the circumstances?
- How do you manage performance?
- How do you reward staff?
- How do you manage feedback?
- What structures will you put in place for meetings: 1–1s, etc.
- What's most important to you?

Step 3: Internal state

What do you want to believe about yourself as a leader? What's most important to you? For example:

- What are the empowering beliefs you wish to have as a leader? For example, 'I can find a solution to every problem.' 'I'm a great motivator of people.'
- In what emotional state do you be as a leader? For example, do you want to be energised or motivated, or do you prefer to be calm and relaxed.
- What's most important to you about being a leader? For example, do you want to focus on developing others or maybe you want to focus on earning a big salary?

///

Well done. That may be the most important thing you ever do in your leadership career. You may find it a challenge to practise all these elements simultaneously. That is normal. Pick one element of your model and focus on that until you are satisfied with your results. Select opportunities where you can practise new strategies. Expect those around you to notice that you are doing things differently. Others may ask to model you as they admire the changes that you are making in your own leadership model!

In Part II of this book you'll have the opportunity to utilise your leadership model in the context of building a high-performing team. World-class leaders know that they can only achieve results through others. They understand that the more successful their teams, the greater their own personal success. Your role as leader is to create a shared vision for your team and to keep them focused, motivated and inspired to deliver. Part II of this book shows you how.

TIP *'Control is not leadership; management is not leadership; leadership is leadership. If you seek to lead, invest at least 50% of your time in leading yourself – your own purpose, ethics, principles, motivation, conduct. Invest at least 20% leading those with authority over you and 15% leading your peers.'*

–Dee Hock, Founder and CEO Emeritus, Visa

PART TWO

TRANSFORMING TEAMS WITH NLP

4
CONSTRUCTING HIGH-PERFORMING TEAMS

'The average team achieves only 63% of the objectives of their strategic plans.'

That was the illuminating statistic produced in the *Harvard Business Review* in an article entitled 'Turning Strategy into Great Performance'. This chapter is all about how to close that gap using NLP. It documents a number of examples of practical applications in a range of different settings. My outcome in this chapter is for you to be able to confidently apply these techniques with your own team or teams. These principles apply to all teams in the business from the leadership and executive team through middle management to front-line teams.

Let's begin by exploring what factors make a high-performing team and examine how to use NLP to develop these factors in your teams.

What makes a successful team?
Of course you can list the knowledge and skills that make for successful team working. However, this doesn't quite answer the question. What's really important is to focus on the way

that the individuals in the team operate together as a successful unit. How do its members behave, what's important to them and what are the informal 'rules' that are adopted? The list of attributes that follows has been modelled from teams that are highly productive and successful.

1. **Shared vision.** A shared vision binds the business together around a common theme. Involve the team members in the planning process as evidence shows that team members are less likely to destroy that which they've helped to create. Teams like this understand their purpose, their individual roles, feel a sense of ownership, and can see how they personally, and as a team, make a difference. Wherever the team is placed in the organisation it knows how it connects to the strategic direction of the business. Individual and team objectives are aligned to the strategy and business plan. There is a 'golden thread' that runs from the top to the bottom of the business, i.e. connecting the strategy and business plan to the target operating model to front-line service plans.

2. **Commitment.** Team members see themselves belonging to the team. They are committed to group goals above and beyond their personal goals and agendas. They are aware of each other's goals and their role in delivering the bigger picture.

3. **Trust.** To create trust, team members need to have shared values. They understand not only what's important to individual team members but also the priorities of the team. They know the 'rules of the game', both formal and informal, and they abide by them. They support each other and generally behave predictably and consistently.

4. **Communication.** Effective teams are aware of how best to communicate with their team members and key stakeholders outside the team. They are flexible and understand how to influence each other to deliver the team's results.

They are open and honest with each other and provide each other with valuable feedback.

5. **Involvement.** Everyone has a role on the team. Despite differences in roles, perspectives and experience, team members feel a sense of partnership with each other. Contributions are respected and expected. True consensus is reached when appropriate.

6. **Development structures.** Senge said that structure influences behaviour. High-performing teams have structures that drive performance. There is a discipline around these structures which helps to make things happen no matter what. These include regular team meetings, one-to-one sessions, appraisals and successful ways of dealing with issues. In my experience, many teams do not have these structures in place or they allow them to fizzle out over time. Where there is a common purpose and direction they last.

7. **Continuous improvement.** This is common sense and yet so rarely happens. It's about reviewing what happened in the past and learning from it. The team has the tools, knowledge and time at their disposal to make continuous improvement really happen. All improvement efforts are done in support of learning and improving the business goals and objectives.

If you already lead a team, you know that the journey to high performance is ongoing. It's the rare team that achieves high performance and just stays there. In my business life, whether I've managed a team within an organisation or, as now, running my own company, it's unusual to keep the same team together for longer than a year. Team members come and go, driven by the needs of the organisation and their own career goals. And every time the members of a team changes, the team needs to regroup and refocus.

///

Exercise 14: What's the best team you've ever experienced?

Think back for a moment to the teams that you have worked in, led or observed. Which teams have stood out for you and why? What was it that differentiated them? What can you learn from their strategies, beliefs, values, behaviours and so on? List the attributes below. Notice the overlap with the points above. Maybe you have discovered some new distinctions.

///

Building team muscle

Developing a high-performing team is like building muscle – if you know what to do and you regularly practise you get the results. I'm going to help you build your team muscle to the point that the following techniques are used automatically, not only by you but also your team members. You are going to explore the potential of meta programmes and values, traditionally NLP Master Practitioner material, to build a high-performing team and to deliver the attributes described at the start of this chapter.

Let's start with meta programmes. What if you could predict how a member of your team will behave in a certain situation based simply on what was said, or you could improve understanding between team members or between you and another team member? Above all, what if you could influence another's behaviour by how you respond?

One of the ways in which it's possible to influence people's behaviour is by framing our communications to match their internal thinking styles. Fom Chapter 3, it's clear that, in order to make sense of the world, we delete, distort and generalise much of the information that comes in through our senses, as we cannot hold onto too many ideas at once. What we delete, and what we pay most attention to, can be thought of as our highest-level ways of absorbing information. They are patterns of thought developed at a very early age – through the influence of parents, teachers and our different experiences. Because these become ingrained into our thinking, we rarely notice them in ourself or in others who share the same patterns. However, we often regard those people with different patterns as stubborn or difficult. Yet they are only running different patterns to the rest of us.

Meta programmes are deep-rooted mental programmes or patterns which automatically filter our experience and guide and direct our thought processes, resulting in significant differences in behaviour from person to person. They define typical patterns in the strategies or thinking styles of an individual, group, company or culture.

Leslie Cameron-Bandler (ex-wife of Richard Bandler) postulated that each person makes specific kinds of deletions, distortions and generalisations which then show up in their behaviour. She identified approximately 60 patterns which she called the 'meta programmes'. Shelle Rose Charvet in *Words that Change Minds* described the meta programmes:

> '...like a door through which we interact with the world. This door has a particular shape and has the power to let only certain things in or out. This may appear to be part of our individual nature, and therefore permanent; in fact the door itself can shift in response to changes in ourselves and our surrounding environment.'

She went onto say that the meta programmes describe the form of our door, what specifically we let in and out in a particular situation. Roger Bailey, a student of Leslie's, reduced the number of patterns from 60 to 14. These are all documented in Shelle's book. In Time Line therapy and the basis of personality, Tad James and Wyatt Woodsmall distill the original 60 programmes down to four basic meta programmes and twenty-one complex meta programmes. There are many similarities between both sets of distilled versions.

Some things to bear in mind about meta programmes:

- As you read the descriptions of meta programmes, if you have difficulty believing someone can live their life this way or if you can't stand someone who lives their life this way, then you are probably at the other end of the spectrum to them.

- Being at one end of the spectrum or in the middle is not better than the others. Each has its positive and negative aspects.

- Your meta programmes may change over time as you learn new information or experience significant events in your life.

- You can identify a person's meta programmes from the language they use and/or their behaviours.

Organisations tend to recruit people in their own likeness, i.e. they have similar meta programmes, and form teams of 'like' people. However, often teams and business units function more effectively with a diverse workforce with a blend of different viewpoints, motivation and capabilities.

I have chosen and adapted five of the meta programmes from Time Line Therapy and the Basis of Personality that are particularly relevant for business. They are to do with motivation, decision-making, perception of relationship, thinking chunk size and reaction to external influences. There are two main styles of behaviour for each meta programme. I will show you how framing your communications with people you want to influence according to their programmes will give you an extra edge.

Now it's time to discover your personal meta programmes. I have developed a questionnaire that will not only assist you to discover your own style but is a useful tool that you can use with your teams.

Exercise 15: What's your style?

Work through the questions below. Here's what to do. For each meta programme there are five questions, each with a choice of two statements. For each question, tick (a) or (b) in the answer grid, depending upon which statement sounds most like you. You then record the number of (a)s and (b)s you have scored and subtract the lowest from the highest score to give you your total for the category. For instance, the example below shows four (a)s for Global and one (b) for Specific under the Chunk Size programme, so my total score for that category would be 3 Global (i.e. 4 – 1).

You will get a score of 1, 3 or 5 for each meta programme. The higher your score, the more intensely you are likely to display characteristics of that style. In contrast, a lower score means that you display some minor characteristics of that style.

Here's a summary table to record your scores. There's a set of example scores to help you.

Meta programme		Score		Score	Final score
Example scores					
Chunk size filter	Global	4	Specific	1	3 Global
Adaptive response filter	Judger	4	Perceiver	1	3 Judger

(Continued)

Meta programme		Score		Score	Final score
Frame of reference filter	Internal	0	External	5	5 External
Relationship filter	Sameness	5	Difference	0	5 Sameness
Direction filter	Towards	1	Away from	4	3 Away from
Your scores					
Chunk size filter	Global		Specific		
Adaptive response filter	Judger		Perceiver		
Frame of reference filter	Internal		External		
Relationship filter	Sameness		Difference		
Direction filter	Towards		Away from		

Following each questionnaire, you'll find a description of each programme as well as a selection of key words that you'd expect each
style to respond well to. You can use these descriptions, not only to
discover more about your own style but also to share information
amongst your team members. Don't worry too much about the
titles of each programme. They are here for reference and if you
wish to research further.

Meta Programme: Chunk size filter

> 1a. I need very little briefing if someone has asked me to do some-
> thing.
> 1b. I need a highly detailed understanding before I can do something.

2a. I prefer to see the big picture.
2b. I prefer to get into the detail.

3a. I tend to listen to others without comment.
3b. I tend to correct others or ask questions on points of detail.

4a. When faced with a challenge, I am open to the broad range of possibilities.
4b. When faced with a challenge I am practical about what can be done.

5a. When I have a task to do I work from a general idea of what needs to be done.
5b. When I have a task to do I make detailed lists of the actions.

Chunk size filter answer grid	a	b
1		
2		
3		
4		
5		
Total →	(Global)	(Specific)
Highest – lowest score =		

Global people

Global people give you the big picture without any of the details. They will describe a situation in random order without using proper nouns or extra modifiers. They are most comfortable with large chunks of information. They make sense of the world in terms of the overall framework of a situation, usually seeing the whole project at once. They can conceive of and work with the parts as necessary, but they usually see them as random bits of the larger framework. They tend to speak in simple sentences with few prepositional phrases. If you present too many details they will ask you what it means or ask you to move on. However, you should expect that they may fill in the details in a different way than you would.

With this style it's best to present the big picture and avoid the small details. Avoid sequences and use generalities.

Key influencing words and phrases include: generally, overview, big picture, framework.

Specific people

Specific people give you all of the small details and chunk down several levels in their explanations. They are comfortable with and able to understand small pieces of data. They talk with and about sequences. They prefer things to be arranged in sequences. When they describe something they will talk about the steps in the event. If interrupted they will often go back to the first step. They are not able to make sense of the larger picture and often have difficulty with priorities.

With this style it's best to break things down into specifics and stress the details. Use a lot of modifiers and proper nouns. Present things in sequences. Avoid generalities and vagueness. Don't expect them to see the big picture.

Key influencing words and phrases include: exactly, specifically, precisely, first – second – then – next.

Meta Programme: Adaptive Response Filter

1a. I prefer a step-by-step planned approach to my work
1b. I prefer to keep my options open for as long as possible

2a. When booking a holiday, I plan every last detail
2b. When planning a holiday I take every day as it comes

3a. I always know there is a right and wrong way to do everything
3b. I believe there are always 'grey' areas in everything

4a. I prefer detailed procedures
4b. I prefer flexibility in my approach

5a. I usually arrive early for appointments
5b. I struggle to arrive for appointments on time and always have an excuse ready

Adaptive Response Filter answer grid	a	b
1		
2		
3		
4		
5		
Total →	(Judger)	(Perceiver)
Highest - lowest score =		

Judgers

Judgers prefer to live in a planned, orderly way, wanting to regulate and order life. They make decisions easily, implement them and move on. Their lifestyle is structured and organised and methodical; they like to have things settled. Sticking to a plan or schedule is very important to them to avoid any last-minute stresses. They are always on time for meetings and appointments.

With judgers it's best to give them clear instructions and guidelines, preferably in a methodical plan. They like to know in advance what to expect without any surprises.

Key influencing words and phrases: orderly, decision, do it now, plan ahead, understand what's happening, let's be clear, certain, milestones, tasks and activities, definite.

Perceivers

Perceivers prefer to live in a flexible, spontaneous way, seeking to experience and understand life. They perform best when they can be flexible and unconstrained. Plans and decisions feel confining to them; they prefer 'to keep their options open' until the absolute last minute. They enjoy and trust their ability to adapt to the demands of a situation and feel energised by last minute pressure. It is difficult to pin them down until there is the threat of a deadline. Even then, a high perceiver will check out to see if it is a 'real' deadline or not! They are often late for meetings and appointments.

With perceivers it's best to keep things fluid. They can respond in the moment and are not disturbed by ambiguity in the way that judgers can be.

Key influencing words and phrases: possibilities, change, different, anything goes, be open, go with the flow, maybe.
When a decision is needed: urgent, set a deadline.

Meta Programme: Frame of reference filter

1a. I am most comfortable when I'm by myself
1b. I am most comfortable with other people

2a. When it comes to decisions, I decide what needs to be done by myself
2b. When it comes to decisions, I rely on other people's opinions to help me decide

3a. At work I drive things through personally
3b I work through others to make things happen

4a. When I think about work, I believe I did it my way
4b. When I think about work I believe I did the best for all concerned

5a. In group activities I make sure I get what I want
5b. In group activities I go along with the others

Frame of reference filter answer grid	a	b
1		
2		
3		
4		
5		
Total →	(Internal)	(External)
Highest – lowest score =		

Internal people

Internal people evaluate things on the basis of what **they** think is appropriate. They provide their own motivation and make their own decisions. They decide what they want to do and how they will go about doing it. They will buy an article of clothing because **they** think it looks good on them, not what the fashion magazines say. They have difficulty accepting other people's direction and feedback. They may gather information from others, but they decide what to do about it. It's useful to emphasise how your goals are aligned with theirs.

It's best to emphasise that the person will ' know inside' what is best. Stress that **they** have to decide. It is best to avoid telling them what other people think; rather, talk about what they think. Help them to clarify their thinking. Ask how you can assist them in deciding.

Key influencing words and phrases include: only you can decide, you decide, it's up to you.

External people

External people tell you that they know because other people or external sources tell them. Other sources provide the information which they then accept. They may describe that incoming information as if that information is a decision. They need external standards and feedback.

These people need to be managed. They need to know what to do and how to do it. They need development feedback and praise. Those with extreme scores (i.e. 5s) will stress if they do not get that feedback.

With these people it's most useful to emphasise what other people think. Give them statistics and data. Tell them what you and significant others think. Tell them when and what to decide. Give them constant feedback and data. Assure them they are doing the right thing. Stress what other people think of the projects and solutions.

Key influencing words and phrases include: other people think, the facts show, this is the way it is, here is some feedback, I will let you know.

Meta Programme: Relationship filter

1a. I would rather perform tasks that are consistent
1b. I would rather perform tasks that are new and challenging

2a. When eating at restaurants, I tend to go to the same places and eat the same food
2b. When eating at restaurants I look for new locations and different types of cuisine

3a. Given the choice, I do things the way I know work
3b. Given the choice, I create a new approach

4a. When I go on holiday, I go to the same places each year
4b. When I go on holiday, I go to new and different places

5a. In meetings I argue on the side of the predictable
5b. In meetings I support different ideas

Relationship filter answer grid	a	b
1		
2		
3		
4		
5		
Total →	(Sameness)	(Difference)
Highest – lowest score =		

Sameness people

Sameness people will first notice the similarities and then notice differences. They may discuss how things have gradually changed over time. They like things to remain relatively the same. They are not comfortable with change unless it occurs slowly and gradually. They talk about how things are the same. They will discuss same or common features or things that have not changed. They tend to use comparatives like 'more', 'less' and 'better'.

With these people it's best to emphasise the continuity, the gradual improvements. They respond best when you stress areas of mutual agreement and the similarities between the current situation and previous situations. Focus on areas of commonality. Frame all differences as gradual or evolutionary improvements. Avoid discussing differences. They will respond better to things that are 'improved, better, or slightly more advanced', but they will resist things that are new.

Key influencing words and phrases include: same, same as, in common, keep the same, maintain, better, same except, evolved, gradual, evolutionary.

Difference people

Difference people will notice things that are different from or mismatch what they have noticed previously. They like change and variety. They don't like static or stable situations. Change doesn't have to be revolutionary, but it does have to happen. Often they are constantly reorganising. Most will notice the differences first, and then the similarities.

In conversation, they will tell you about the differences between things or situations. They will often use words like 'new, changed, different, revolutionary'.

It's most useful to emphasise the improvements and only then mention areas of continuity. Expect that they will demand some change. Play down the similarities. They tend to respond best when you first stress how things are different and only then mention areas of continuity. Focus on new and creative solutions. Emphasise differences.

Key influencing words and phrases include: new, different, changed, unusual.

Meta Programme: Direction filter

1a. I prefer to take risks to win
1b. I prefer to avoid risks to not lose

2a. When I need to do something unpleasant I get it done to make room for other things

2b. When I need to do something unpleasant I put it off until the last minute

3a. Regarding activities, I get involved and have fun

3b. Regarding activities, I avoid participating because of the possible consequences

4a. In social situations I enjoy meeting new people

4b. In social situations, I avoid meeting new people unless they approach me first

5a. People describe me as always thinking about the possibilities

5b. People describe me as risk averse

Direction filter answer grid	a	b
1		
2		
3		
4		
5		
Total →	(Towards)	(Away From)
Highest – lowest score =		

Towards people

There are two fundamental reasons why anyone does anything – to move towards something (outcomes or goals or to attain certain things), or to move away from something (discomfort, pain, danger, insecurity). Towards people are motivated to have, achieve, get or attain. They talk about what they want, about people things, situations they want to include. They tend to set priorities and are good at maintaining them. Sometimes they have difficulty in recognising what should be avoided and they are frequently oblivious to what is not working or what is going wrong. They respond best to carrots and incentives.

With these people, it's best to emphasise goals and what they can get, attain, or achieve. However, it's important to be aware that they may be either blind to or ignore potential problems. It's best to present projects and solutions in a way that emphasises how they will help them achieve what they want. They want to know what the projects will do for them. They respond best when you stress what you can do to help them attain or achieve their outcomes, especially if you emphasise how both sides are trying to achieve the same things.

Key influencing words and phrases include: get, attain, achieve, have, attract, include, obtain.

Away from people

Away from people are motivated to move away from, steer clear of, or get rid of. They talk about what they don't want, what they want to avoid or steer clear of. They often have difficulty maintaining goal focus and managing priorities. They are easily distracted by negative situations. They respond best to threats and sticks.

With these people, it's best to emphasise threats and problems. These threats and problems need to be real and believable. This is their home territory, so they'll be quite used to evaluating the seriousness of threats.

They respond best when you explain how you can help them avoid what they don't want, presenting projects and solutions in a way that emphasises how they will help them avoid hassles. Anticipate potential problems and assure them that these will be minimised or avoided. Have plenty of answers ready for questions about what can go wrong. In discussions, it's often necessary to control them by always raising their problems.

Key influencing words and phrases include: avoid, repulsed by, steer clear of, keep away from, exclude, get rid of, not have.

What did you learn?

Did you have any surprises with your scores when you read the descriptions? What was the most important learning for you? Maybe you experienced a few 'light-bulb' moments as your scores helped you to unravel why some of your relationships at work are easy with those who are similar to you and more of a challenge with those who are unlike you. The key influencing words and phrases are valuable in starting to consciously work out what to say to another person in your team or even your boss! For example, what do you do if you are a high score judger managing a high score perceiver? You may start by pointing out all the possibilities in a new project to motivate your staff member and get them engaged. However, when you need completion of work you are equally likely to need to give them a tight deadline as that's the only way they'll make a decision and get things finalised. If you don't understand what's going on it can be extremely frustrating for a judger manager.

In the example given in the scoring table on pages 91 and 92, how would you manage this person to get the best out of them? Their high sameness (5) and away-from (3) scores mean that they would most enjoy repetitive, low-risk work. Any sudden change to routine would be a challenge for them. Their judger (3) score also means that they enjoy structure and process. It would be important to put them in the right kind of role to play to their strengths. For example, a finance or IT role may suit them well. The score of external (5) also tells us that they will require a lot of feedback from you as their manager to know that they are on track. This person would need careful managing during a period of change. It would be important to focus on what's staying the same before pointing out anything that is changing.

You can begin to see how the meta programmes give you an instruction guide not only for what plays to your strengths but also how to get the best out of your team members and other important stakeholders.

How to use meta programmes with your teams

Use the questionnaire with your team so each member of the team can build their flexibility in communicating with their colleagues. If that is not possible you have enough information from the descriptions of each programme to work out which combination of programmes each person in your team is running. It is likely that those team members you get on best with are those who share similar patterns to you. You are likely to have the biggest challenges with team members who have radically different styles to you. For example, if you are an 'external' team leader who likes to collaborate you may be stretched by a high 'internal' team member who has strong views of their own and resists your ideas. Or if you are a 'global' boss you may be frustrated by a 'specific' team member who needs you to explain everything in lots of detail to them.

To build the highest-performing team it's essential that all the team members understand each other's profiles and can build their flexibility in dealing with each other. If you can influence another by speaking their language then they are much more likely to listen to your ideas, suggestions and ultimately achieve their potential. Much time is wasted by team members who do not listen to each other or do not understand where the other person is coming from. In the examples above, imagine how useful it would have been to know exactly how to influence the 'internal' staff member to listen and accept ideas or to be able to communicate to the 'specific' member in a way that meant they would deliver back exactly what was needed instead of wasting time through many unnecessary iterations of the process.

The human graph

At The Change Corporation we have used this exercise in many different situations, from leadership development programmes to team building events. It works really well with groups of 12 or more people. If you have a smaller team, de-brief directly from the completed questionnaires. It has been demonstrated time and time again that this is a 'light-bulb' moment for staff who suddenly understand why they haven't been able to communicate effectively with other members of their team – or even their boss! For example, we run a 'Start Supervising' programme within a large county council. This is a development programme for new managers who are managing staff for the first time. We have now used this exercise with over 300 of their staff. It is the exercise that gets the best feedback from the whole event as it provides new managers with the 'key' to unlocking different behavioural patterns in their new teams.

We take an hour to run this exercise and conduct a thorough de-brief. Each person completes the questionnaire. We use a large room where there is space for staff to stand around the sides. Six cards are made up – two marked with a '5', two marked with the number '3' and two marked with the number '1' – and fixed along two opposite sides of the room where they can be clearly seen in this order: '5,3,1,1,3,5'.

Once the group has completed the questionnaire I go through their scores, focusing on one meta programme at a time. For example, with the Chunk Size Filter meta programme (i.e global/specific), I ask everyone who has either a 5/3/1 global score to stand by the appropriate number along one side of the room. Then those with a specific score do the same thing along the opposite side of the room.

Once all the staff are in position I de-brief using the following questions:

- What do you notice about the distribution of the group? For example, is there a high percentage of staff in one particular category? What does that mean for the group?

- Are there any people with maximum scores, i.e. people with a score of 5? How does their behaviour play out in the team?

- What other communication issues does this team face?

- How specifically can the 'globals' work more effectively with the 'specifics' and visa versa? (Reference back to the key influencing words and phrases.)

- What else is of interest?

I then go through the other four programmes in the same way. Each person also prepares their own personal actions from what they have learned. Of course, it's important that everyone realises that they won't always have the opportunity to get another person to complete the questionnaire! They learn that, by observing behaviour and language, they can soon become 'experts' at identifying what meta programmes other people are running. For example, if someone appears stubborn, inflexible, doesn't like feedback and is unwilling to defer to another viewpoint, they may well be running an 'internal' filter.

Other applications of meta programmes

- Employing high-performing individuals

   This works on two levels – understanding the 'ideal' meta programme profile for a vacant role and appointing the person who closely fits that profile (taking into account other essential requirements as well). Also, understanding where there is a gap in the team profile and employing to fill that gap too.

- Coaching/staff development

   When you are working one to one with a team member, knowing their profile will enable you to assist them to reach their potential as quickly as possible.

- Career counselling

  Understanding someone's profile will help you point them in the direction of a career that suits them and that they will perform well in.

- Corporate culture diagnosis and change management

  Because people tend to hire in their own image, organisations do tend to have a preponderance of one programme or another. They may need to shift to other patterns to function most effectively.

- Negotiations

  Meta programmes can be used for understanding the needs and communication style of all parties. They will also allow you to present your proposals in ways that your partners in negotiation can best accept.

- Learning and development

  Knowing the meta programmes of your delegates will again allow you to present the learning in a way that they will best understand and use.

- Sales and marketing

  Assessing the meta programmes of your customers will enable you to present your products and proposals in a way that they will appreciate and value.

Using meta programmes to get better results

A global electronics organisation has been running its development programme for aspiring leaders for five years. The aim of the programme is to prepare junior managers for their first leadership role and to benefit from a global networking opportunity. Most of the participants are in highly technical roles and many have come from an engineering or scientific background. Though very intelligent, many of them have little experience in dealing with the day-to-day people issues in a busy team. We were asked to run modules on communications and leadership skills to build the delegate's flexibility and capability in dealing with staff. The modules contain an extensive NLP segment including meta programmes.

Here are some specific examples where staff used meta programmes with those around them with impressive results:

- In South Africa, a manager described how he had used 'global–specific' and 'sameness–difference' in strategic discussions to help facilitate agreement and understanding of the topics under discussion.

- In Europe, one young manager discovered that many of his colleagues and team members were high 'internals'. As he is an 'external' this discovery helped him to understand why he had been having a challenge in getting them to listen to his ideas about improving the way the office ran. He found he could influence them more easily on a one-by-one basis, especially if he used phrases like 'only you can decide if this makes sense, try it out and let me know, what do you think?'

- In Asia, a female manager used meta programmes to influence her boss more effectively. She is very specific and he is very global. She used to get very frustrated when she prepared lots of detail for him and he was dismissive of what she had done. Now she spends time preparing an overview for him with the key points summarised and finds that she gets both his attention and the outcome that she wants.

- In Eastern Europe, one team leader keeps a matrix of the meta programmes for each of his team members. As he finds out more information he records it on the matrix. This helps him communicate far more effectively and empathetically with each of his team members and he finds that they are more motivated to improve the results of the whole team. He said that it reminds him that an 'unimportant' detail for him as a 'global' manager can be massively important to a 'specific' member of his team. He also uses the tool to coach his team about his own preferences so they know how to deal with him. He said that NLP has increased his self-awareness enormously.

As you use meta programmes you will notice what a difference they make to those you work with (and for those at home too). The possibilities are endless for communicating in just the 'right' way. You can make a big difference to the results of your team as members are more motivated to succeed and are better able to attain the best results first time around.

Now, let's now move onto exploring how to align the values of your team members to take team performance to a world-class level.

The power of team values

Our values are instilled in us at an early age, mostly before the age of seven. At this age your surroundings are imprinted upon you with little of your own filtering. For example, your values will be influenced by the values of your parents, close family, environment, school, and everything and everyone else that touches your life. If you want to find out what your values are, then ask yourself what was important to those around you when you were growing up as it's likely that you have adopted many of their standards.

Values are important in the context of a high-performing team because they determine why you do what you do. Your values determine the way you think and how you behave. They are the reason that you do what you do. They motivate you to take action and they are the means by which you evaluate yourself after the event, and decide if you did a good job – or, indeed, the right thing. Your values also provide your moral code, so if you feel uncomfortable about anything you've done it's likely to be due to a conflict of values.

In other words, your values are what are most important to you – and yet they are largely unconscious. You know they are there, though, because whenever you start to feel uneasy about something it is due to a values conflict within you. For example, if you're unhappy at work then one strong possibility is that you are experiencing a values conflict somewhere along the line. The trouble is that as your values are largely unconscious, you do not know what they are. As a result, you may drift into careers and teams that are not aligned with your values. You often discover this after the fact, when there is a clash between what is going on in the team around you and how you feel. This manifests as an inner conflict that could lead to you feeling unhappy or even ill – and often you don't know why. Just imagine, then, if you were able to elicit and align the values of your team. You would have a motivated team all focused in the same direction. Members would be prepared to cooperate as it would be clear to them how what they do fits into the aligned team values. It would save much discussion and wrangling and provide space for high performance to flourish.

Eliciting team values

I am going to show you how to work with your team to elicit, share and align their values for working in a high-performing team. This is a very powerful process, and it is also a lengthy one and should be completed in one go. It also needs a strong facilitator as values are an emotive subject. It is not unusual for team members to disagree with each other during the early part of this process. It's important to set some clear ground rules. The principles or pre-suppositions of NLP are a good starting point as they recognise and respect different models of the world. All team members have to be committed to the outcome and to take responsibility for achieving it.

//

Exercise 16: Aligning team values

Step 1: Elicitation of individual team values

One by one, each team member should have their team values elicited. This should be done whilst the whole team is there in order for other team members to get an understanding of what motivates each of them individually. It is helpful for everyone to understand that there are many different models of the world within the team. It can be a moment of enlightenment, similar to eliciting meta programmes, when members realise 'oh that's why you react like that...'. If you have a very large team it is feasible to prepare individual values off-line then bring them along to a team meeting.

You begin by asking each team member in turn, 'What's important to you about working in this team?' Write down the words that the person says and do not suggest any answers, as these are likely to be your own values. In NLP, the words being listened for are called 'nominalisations'. A nominalisation is a verb (process word) which has been transformed into a static or abstract noun. For example, communicate has become communication, or relate has become relationship. Also, listen out for answers such as 'working with intelligent people'. That is not a nominalisation. In this case the facilitator would ask: 'What does working with intelligent people do or get for you?' The answer might be: 'It gives me inspiration at work.' Inspiration is the value.

You continue with the questioning, even when the answers start to dry up. This is because conscious values come out first, as they are at surface level. Unconscious values are those that we are least aware of, and are likely to come out later and may prove to be the most important of all the values identified.

An example of a team member's list of values might look like this:

- Inspiration
- Integrity
- Recognition
- Success
- Creativity
- Communication
- Security
- Fun
- Honesty
- Reward
- Recognition
- Learning

Step 2: Hierarchy of values

Next you ask the team member to pick their top eight values and rank them in order of priority. Then you should re-write the list on a flip-chart.

Step 3: Find out what the values mean

Then explore what each value means to that individual. It will soon become clear that the same value means different things to different people. This is also very illuminating. For example, inspiration to one person might mean being inspired by the team creating new ways of working, whilst to another it might mean having all the latest technology to work within the team. This can also be a lively part of the exercise as people dispute meanings. At the end of the day they are all right answers. However, agreement on meanings does need to be reached at step 5. It's also important to establish the evidence criteria to know the value has been fulfilled. For example, you would ask 'what has to happen for you to be inspired?'

Step 4: Move onto team values

Once everyone has had their individual values elicited it's time to move on to the team values. It's important that the team has agreed at the start to have a democratic process of agreeing the team values. You will need to have everyone's flip charts around the room at this point. Then delete all the duplicate values so each value appears only once. Give each team member x 8 votes. Each person marks their top 8 values with a dot. This makes it easy for you to count up the dots against each value. The 8 values are then written up on a new flip chart – from highest to lowest score. If any values have the same score then the team agrees the order.

Step 5: Agree meanings and evidence criteria

You then go through each value and get agreement on what it means for the team and how they will know when they have it. The team will begin to self-regulate at this point as they recognise their own values playing out in the discussions.

Final step: Score current performance

The team then scores each of the 8 values against current performance levels. They do this by each person giving a score of 1–10 (10 is high) against each value. For example, if the team has openness on their list and you believe they are not open at the moment you would give a low score of, say, 4. Average scores are then calculated for each value.

0–4	High risk area for the team
5–7	Medium risk area for the team
8–10	Low risk area for the team

An action plan is then agreed to move towards a score of 10 for each value.

A large global contract services organisation that operates in the healthcare sector

This company has 710 employees and operates in the health-care sector. In 2009, the Change Corporation was asked to run an NLP Business Practitioner for their HR leadership team of eight people. We designed a 4-day programme which included a team values elicitation. The values elicitation was done as per the exercise detailed here and was a real eye opener for the team. The team members each came up with their own lists of values first. Fortunately, there was a lot of overlap between individual values and so it became a relatively quick and straightforward task to pull out the team values. The final list of values and the agreed meanings were as follows:

- OPPORTUNITY: For professional growth and intellectual challenge for the individual and the team

- COMMUNICATION: Open, transparent, timely, clear, honest, using an effective mode with strong inter-personal skills

- COLLABORATIVE: Working together in a supportive manner to achieve

- SUPPORT: Acceptance of difference and provide assistance to each other

- TRUST: The belief in each other

- ACHIEVEMENT: A job well done with a successful outcome

- RECOGNITION: Being valued.

- RESPECT: Reciprocal appreciation of the skills and values individuals bring to the team

Here's a quote from one of the team members evaluating the impact of this exercise:

'The impact of this exercise raised awareness and consideration of our differences and similarities. The negotiation process to get to these shared team values also created a shared sense of team spirit and a uniform view of the way the team wanted to interact and be perceived within the wider organisation. Linked to strategic objectives and individual goals, the exercise went a long way towards improving the way that we worked as a team. This was evidenced through a more collaborative approach and improved relationships.' Karen, HR Manager

Pulling it all together

What's the difference between a high-performing team and an average team? Often staff in both teams will have the technical skills to be able to do their jobs. It's relatively easy to teach the knowledge and skills required to perform a role. That then presupposes that something else makes the difference. At this level it's the team members' behaviour and interpersonal skills that make the difference. According to Marshall Goldsmith, these are the most significant changes you can make as a team leader. Savvy team leaders pay attention to helping team members become more aware of differences and similarities within the team so the team can play to its strengths. They also help build awareness and flexibility of behaviour and alignment of goals and commitment. Meta programmes and values alignment are key tools at a team leader's disposal to make this happen. Let's remind ourselves of the attributes of a high-performing team that were discussed at the start of this chapter:

- Shared vision

- Commitment

- Trust

- Communication

- Involvement

- Development structures

- Continuous improvement

Certainly, values alignment will make a major contribution towards a shared vision because the team is agreed on what is most important for them to deliver results. Values work also goes a long way to building commitment and trust within the team. Trust in particular is an elusive quality to create. You as the team leader can't force your team to be supportive and trusting – it's a natural result of sharing ideas and agreeing about what's important to the team.

Improved communication is developed through flexibility and increased awareness of others. This comes from understanding why people have different models of the world and why they do what they do. Flexible communicators can get the best out of everyone around them. Good communicators will also maximise the involvement of others as they know how to play to the team's strengths. Both of these attributes are developed through an awareness and utilisation of meta programmes.

Development structures again will survive and prosper in the long term if they are seen as important to the team and the whole team signs up to them. It just doesn't work if team members find one-to-ones useful but their team leader is too busy to make the necessary time available. This has to be part of the values defined by the team in the beginning. That way, if team members renege on their commitments they will be self-regulated by other team members. A motivated team is also one where learning and improvement will take place as each team member takes pride in high performance and wishes to retain that status. Open and honest feedback is also important here and this will be dealt with in the next chapter.

Building a high-performing team is not an easy task. However, if you're a team leader who is up to the challenge, then consciously focus on developing these attributes through the understanding of meta programmes in the team and the alignment of values. Revisit these commitments regularly and see what develops. I guarantee a rewarding journey to high performance.

 Take one person at a time in your team and focus on recognising their meta programmes. I guarantee you'll soon be doing it unconsciously.

5
ENCOURAGING CREATIVITY IN YOUR TEAM

Why is creativity important to high-performing teams?

'There is nothing more powerful than a new idea. An idea can be created out of nothing except an inspired mind. An idea weighs nothing. Yet it can be transferred to billions around the world at the speed of light for virtually no cost. And yet an idea, when received by a prepared mind, can have an extraordinary impact. It can re-shape the mind's view of the world. It can dramatically alter the behaviour of the receiver. It can cause the mind to pass on the idea to others. In fact, the only way that mankind has ever evolved was through the communication and adoption of a better idea.' (www.ted.com)

Creativity is the life-blood of a high-performing team because it enables that team to differentiate itself from the rest of the pack and it builds a culture of continuous improvement. A team that doesn't create will eventually become a dinosaur and die. Creativity does not necessarily mean a huge change; in some teams it may be a simple process efficiency that makes a difference to staff and customers alike. The important issue is to develop an environment in your team where creativity will flourish, whatever the scale and scope of the project. This chapter shows how to develop that environment using NLP. It also explores two famous modelling projects with Walt Disney and Metallica so you can learn how to use their creativity secrets with your own team.

Creativity is becoming increasingly important as businesses all over the world struggle to respond to industry changes and new competitive challenges. It is also becoming more important in government, where there is huge pressure to produce efficiency savings. Importantly, creativity contributes to the business's capacity to achieve its goals. It involves the deliberate introduction of new methods, structures, processes or products to improve its ability to conduct its business. This means coming up with creative improvements and then driving them through the business to ensure their implementation.

Learning to tap into our creativity

Many people have problems getting to a state of creativity. By that I mean the state of mind that allows you to be free to innovate. You may feel the same too. However, even though creativity may seem magical, you can learn to be better at it. Of course, some people have a greater disposition and skill to be able to do it, but that is nothing more than taking the time to develop this skill. You have learned from NLP that results are state driven, so to be better at creativity you need to be in the 'right' creative state. The following exercise shows you how. You can use it alone or with your team when you have a problem to solve.

Exercise 17: Accessing creative states

Step 1: Learn to get into a complete state of relaxation

The state of relaxation helps you to get into an 'alpha' state. This is where alpha brain waves are dominant, allowing you to access a range of different capabilities, including creativity. By learning to relax you are learning to bring out the best in yourself.

Step 2: Anchoring

There are people who would not normally describe themselves as creative, yet they can remember a time in the past when they were so. In NLP, it is believed that powerful positive states from the past, like creativity, can be accessed and used in the now. In NLP, this process is called anchoring. In NLP, it's possible to go back to a time in the past when you were creative and re-access that state in the now. By reconnecting with this experience of the past, you literally send your neurology back in search of this pathway, re-igniting it and generating a higher level of familiarity with it. It's like working a muscle – the more you train it the more it develops! To do this it's important to remember a specific time in the past when you were creative. If you are doing this with your team, each member would think about a specific memory. You then imagine floating back into your body at that time, seeing what you saw, hearing what you heard and feeling what you felt. It's really important to ramp up any feelings associated with this experience. As you do this, you will notice yourself fully associating into the state of creativity again. Once you have re-accessed this state you can use it for whatever purpose you need. You can do this either individually or with your whole team at the start of a session when you need them to be at their most creative!

At the end of this exercise is a script for a creative relaxation exercise incorporating anchoring back to a previous state of creativity. You can download an mp3 version from my web site (www.thechangecorporation.com).

Step 3: Create a 'polarity' mindset

Polarity thinking allows you to break away from standard responses that people produce to problems and helps to access innovative and unique approaches. Here are a couple of techniques for accessing polarity. They are not from NLP directly and I have used them widely in the past with groups with surprisingly unique results.

- **The Wrong Way.** Here instead of generating good ideas, the group deliberately tries to generate poor ideas or discuss ways of making the problem worse. For example, if you are trying to solve recurring customer complaints about service, ask 'How could every customer who contacts us be infuriated? What could be done to ensure that no first-time customer would ever want to buy from us a second time?' By concentrating on poor customer service, the focus is on the service issues which matter most to customers, in turn generating ideas which are better poised to solve the problem.
- **Risky Options.** Group members may be afraid to suggest unusual or potentially 'risky' solutions to problems. To inject levity into the process, offer a prize to the group member who poses the riskiest option of all. After a short period of silence and more than a little mumbling some surprising ideas may emerge!
- **The Challenge.** Here the problem is made deliberately worse than it really is, forcing it to be addressed from a different perspective. For example, you are trying to reduce order processing time from six working days to three working days. In order to focus more aggressively on the problem, ask the group to consider what would happen if order volume increased to 1000%. What new systems would have to be put in place to address the problem? Exaggerating the problem forces the group to think creatively about solutions

Script for a creative relaxation exercise

'Just make yourself comfortable in your chair. That's right. Can you feel the weight of your feet on the floor? Can you hear the sound of my voice? Just go ahead now and close your eyes. Be aware of the weight of your eyelids. Allow your eyelids to relax so much that you might be surprised to find that you couldn't open them even if you tried. And again, be aware of the weight of your feet on the floor. And, as you listen to my voice I want you to notice that every time I pause you can take the opportunity to relax even more than you are right now. I want you to let yourself go down to that depth of relaxation that's right for you. Not too deep, not too light. Just deep enough that you get the best results.

As you're sitting in your chair I want you to remember a time when you were really creative, a specific time. Imagine floating back into your body at that moment, looking through your own eyes. See what you saw, hear what you heard and really get back in touch with the feelings of being creative. Turn up the brightness, the sounds and especially the feelings of that whole experience. I want you to know that your creativity is there for you to use whenever you need it. You can easily connect with those abilities that you have by simply going back to a time in the past when you were creative.

And then, I want you to know that you can use this creativity now to reach new peaks, new challenges, new things that you are able to achieve with total ease. And, when you're ready come back into the room and open your eyes. Welcome back!'

Learning from world-class creators

You learned in Chapter 3 how to model. Now I want to explore the outcomes of two famous NLP modelling studies from Walt Disney and Metallica to discover what else there is to learn from two very different sources of creativity.

Walt Disney

Robert Dilts, a personal contributor to the field of NLP, wrote of his Disney modelling project in the first volume of his book *Strategies of Genius*. He felt that Walt Disney's ability to connect his innovative creativity with successful business strategy and popular appeal qualified him as a genius in the field of entertainment.

Dilts discovered that one of the major elements of Disney's unique genius was his ability to explore something from a number of different roles working in coordination with each other. He identified three roles which became known as the Dreamer, the Realist and the Critic. Each role involved a different style of thinking and behaving. Dilts wrote:

> 'Creativity as a total process involves the coordination of these three sub-processes: dreamer, realist and critic. A dreamer without a realist cannot turn ideas into tangible expressions. A critic and a dreamer without a realist just become stuck in a perpetual conflict. The dreamer and a realist might create things, but they might not achieve a high degree of quality without a critic. The critic helps to evaluate and refined the products of creativity.'

The Dreamer

Disney the Dreamer could visualise extraordinary scenarios, for new business projects as well as animated films. In Dreamer mode, Disney had the ability to immerse himself in his imagination, to the exclusion of everything else. When Walt was deep in thought he would stare fixedly at some point in space for long periods of time. Anyone with hypnotic training will recognise several classic indicators of a trance state. This is similar to the process to the one you experienced in Exercise 17.

Questions to bring out your Dreamer:

- What do you want to change?
- What do you want to achieve?

- What excites and inspires you about your idea?

- If you could do anything you like – what would you create? How would it look/sound/feel? What would it get for you, your team and your customer/s?

The Realist

Disney wasn't just a creative thinker. As a committed Realist, he made things happen. He had a phenomenal ability to motivate and coordinate teams of diverse workers to bring his dreams to life. Without the Realist's practical thinking and energetic activity, Disney's achievements would have remained no more than a twinkle in the Dreamer's eye.

Questions to bring out your Realist:

- What resources do you need to make this happen – people, money, materials and technology?

- What are the deliverables?

- What's your plan?

- What obstacles will you face?

- How will you get round them?

The Critic

Disney the Critic subjected every piece of work to rigorous scrutiny. For example, every foot of rough animation was projected on the screen for analysis, and every foot was drawn and redrawn until it was the best that could be done.The Critic provided a valuable feedback loop in the creative process.

Questions to bring out your Critic:

- What's different about this idea?

- Is it cost effective?

- Who are our competitors?

- What reaction will we get from our customers?

- Is this the best I/we can do?

- What would make it even better?

How I can use Disney's creativity strategy

Disney's approach to creativity isn't limited to animated feature films – it's a strategy for success in any creative endeavour. Every creative project needs to incorporate the three aspects of creative imagination, practical action and critical refinement. As an individual, you need to have some capability in all three roles or have people around you who can play the roles you cannot. Most of us are naturally stronger in one or two roles, and decidedly weaker in a third. The first step is having the self-awareness to recognise this. And the next is to commit to developing the skills necessary for that role or bringing in others who can fulfill them.

For example, I'm naturally very comfortable as a Dreamer and a Realist. I'm a writer, creative thinker and a planner. However, I'm not so good at managing the risks around my projects. I get carried away and need a Critic to rein me in. For each project you work on, make sure you cover all three bases. Timing is also important. Allow the Dreamer to finish the first draft or prototype before introducing the Critic too early. Otherwise, the Critic will pull the work to shreds before it has even been put together! Another classic problem is the Dreamer who is great at creative thinking but lacks the Realist's focus on action. And so on – the key is to achieve a dynamic balance between the different roles. You can only get so far by trying to play all three roles yourself. You can achieve much more by partnering with people whose natural strengths complement your own. If you're a hard-headed Realist, team up with Dreamers and Critics.

Exercise 18: Which are you?

Do you recognise the Dreamer, the Realist, and the Critic in your-self? Ask yourself the following questions:

Which role(s) do you feel most comfortable with?

Which role(s) do you find most challenging?

How are the three roles represented in your current team?

Which roles could do with developing within the team?

(Adapted from *The Secret of Walt Disney's Creativity* by Mark McGuinness, poet, creative coach and co-founder of lateralaction.com)

Metallica creativity

In 2006, Silvia Hartmann modelled the rock group Metallica who have sold over 100 million albums.

Here, in essence, is what they did. They would 'jam' to-gether, try out music and lyrics and record everything. They recorded everything in order to pick out the events that had an 'extraordinary' quality about them – even if it was just one thing in the randomness of the session. Sylvia describes these events as 'like a rock that sticks out of a smooth stream of nothingness – a POW! ZAP! WOW! moment'. It is these events that create the physiological response in the body and connect to our emotions.

Then the group would go back over everything that had happened, searching for the extraordinary events that they felt good about, that made a real impact on the band members. They would isolate these events and practise them repeatedly. The final stage was to link them together in a single song. Once enough exceptional events were isolated, the rest was relatively simple.

Hartmann said:

> 'This is like placing enough jig saw puzzle pieces together and you know the picture is a face, and you can recognise it, even though more than half is still missing. You then also know what the missing pieces have to be, and it is easy to find them and add them in.'

In essence this is the process Metallica was using:

- Generate as much material as possible
- Review the material and localise the exceptional events
- Isolate and lock down these events
- Use the events discovered as a new second level jump off point for generating further material
- Review, localise, isolate and lock down further exceptional events

- Group the events according to their energetic flavour and matching relationships

- Use the group of events to understand the finished product, and fill in the blanks accordingly

The interesting discovery that Hartmann made was that, despite there being easier ways of being creative, the only real talent required was to be able to spot the exceptional events, to have a feedback device and to be aware enough to know when something impactful had happened. It's an extraordinary observation that even that basic skill is actually quite rare in the general public, or perhaps it is simply that most of us don't appreciate the power of our own emotional energy responses or gut feel to outside events to guide us in the right direction.

How you can use Metallica's strategy

As I read through the Metallica case study it reminded me of brainstorming techniques. What's important is that the team is in a creative state and free to be random about what they come up with. Much of the 'product' will be rubbish and yet there will be those odd moments when someone in the team has a 'flow' moment that the rest of the team can build upon. What's important is a focus on creativity, idea generation and a non-judgemental atmosphere. Here are some traditional and more off-the-wall brainstorming techniques:

- **Classic brainstorming.** Using classic brainstorming, the group focuses its undivided attention on an issue for a limited period of time – probably between 30 and 90 minutes. The idea is to generate as many solutions to the problem as possible while someone writes them all down. Quantity of ideas, not quality, is what counts here and criticism is not allowed at this time. Afterwards, the 'flow' ideas can be identified and built upon.

- **What if?** Using this technique, each member of the group is asked to pose at least three 'what if' questions about the topic being discussed. Suppose the objective is to reduce employee turnover. 'What if every employee was given a bonus at the three-year mark?' or 'What if flexi-time was instituted?' or 'What if employees were surveyed to find out what their likes and dislikes are about their work?' The 'what if'technique enables consideration of hypothetical perspectives that are not part of current thinking. Again, the best ideas are built on.

- **Metaphors.** A metaphor is a word or phrase that symbolises something other than its literal meaning. For example, if you are seeking ways to energise the sales team, visualise it as a football squad, how would its performance be improved? By applying metaphors to current processes, a fresh outlook on the problems may be gained.

- **Word associations.** Instead of trying to generate concrete solutions or ideas, here the group simply generates whatever words or phrases come to mind when facing a problem. If discussing ways to improve customer service, the group might generate phrases like: 'smiles', 'reward', 'colourful', 'opening hours', 'phone system' and so on. Later, these key phrases can be used to develop new ideas and strategies.

- **The hunter.** With this technique, group members scan through the pages of newspapers, magazines, speeches, literature and products in search of random ideas that might have a bearing on the problem at hand. This technique can be used equally well with individuals and small groups.

Corporate flow

As a change consultant, one of my clients was a large global electronics manufacturer, struggling in the economic climate. They needed to attract new business fast and make efficiencies throughout the business. I project-managed a team who trained a global army of 1000 project managers in 10 weeks to help them lead a vast range of efficiency projects. The efficiency ideas were generated throughout the business at 'Idea Generation Workshops' which we designed and facilitated. The purpose of the workshops was to get front-line staff to come up with ideas for cost savings. These were fast moving workshops lasting two hours. Staff volunteered to attend which guaranteed motivated delegates. There were no restrictions on the ideas they could generate – the only principle was that each idea had to be able to save money. At the workshop a variety of brainstorming techniques were used to generate ideas. Once that was finished the ideas were sifted to identify the potential 'flow moments' that offered the most potential. These were then passed to the project managers for development into full-blown business cases and then the final investment areas were agreed.

NLP strategies for lateral thinking

Lateral thinking is talked about a lot in the context of creativity. Edward de Bono has written many books on the subject, and is regarded by many as a leading authority in the field of creative thinking, innovation and the direct teaching of thinking as a skill. You would use lateral thinking when you want to move from one known idea to creating new ideas. It's all about thinking out of the box and coming up with unique ideas.

In NLP, the 'Hierarchy of Ideas' is a linguistic tool that allows the user to move through and between different levels of abstraction from the vague and ambiguous to the concrete and specific. Albert Einstein said that: 'Problems cannot be solved at the same level of awareness that created them'.

The 'Hierarchy of Ideas' assists you to move into different levels of awareness for problem-solving purposes. The basic principle is that, as you get more and more abstract with your language and concepts, you deal with larger and larger chunks of data. As you get more concrete, you deal with smaller and smaller chunks of data. Imagine an hierarchy of ideas or concepts with the most abstract and all-embracing at the top and the most concrete at the bottom. When you 'chunk up', you move up the hierarchy of ideas. When you 'chunk down', you get more and more concrete.

The Hierarchy of Ideas

Let's take the car as an example. The word 'car' is at a particular level of abstraction. If you want more information about the type of car, price, reliability, etc. you need to begin to 'chunk down' on the word 'car' as you move to a lower level of abstraction – something more concrete and specific. You can do this by asking questions such as:

- What are examples of this?

- What specifically?

So if the subject of the communication was 'car' you might ask 'What type of car specifically?' and chunk down to Ford. If you require further detail you could chunk down one more level by asking something like 'What model of Ford specifically?' and you might get a response of 'Capri' as in the example overleaf (that's showing my age!).

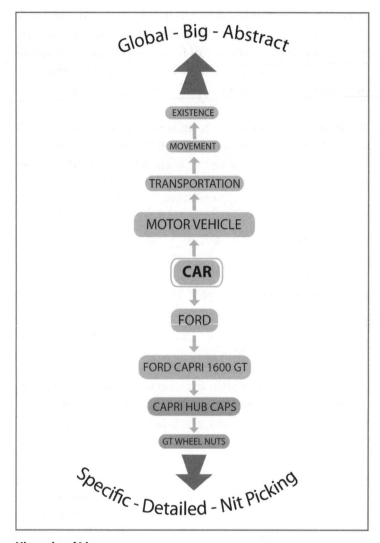

Hierarchy of Ideas

In this particular example you've chunked down on the class or category of the subject in question. An alternative available to you to gain specificity is to chunk down on parts, i.e. instead of chunking down from 'car' to 'manufacturer to model', you could also have chunked down from 'car' to 'engine' to 'spark plug'. With each increasing level of specificity you are moving down through the hierarchy of ideas, down through levels of abstraction. Detail and specificity are useful under certain circumstances and for certain applications.

At the other end of the spectrum there are circumstances and applications which are better served by taking an overall or 'big picture' view. When you've been 'down in the detail' and you want to move up to take look at the 'big picture' or, if you like, take a 'bird's eye view' of things, you chunk up.

Questions that you can ask to assist you in chunking up include:

- What is this an example of?
- For what purpose?
- What is your intention?

If you return to your previous example of 'car' and chunk up one level by asking the question 'What is this an example of?' you may chunk up to 'motor vehicle'. If you chunk up one more level by asking the question again you may chunk up to 'vehicle'. Chunk up again and you may arrive at 'transportation' and eventually to 'movement' or even 'existence'. Each time you chunk up one level you move to a higher level of abstraction and I'm pretty sure you would agree that 'existence' is a far more abstract concept than 'car'.

So what, you might ask yourself! Well, chunking is a good concept for a leader to understand, because many communication difficulties involve mismatched chunk sizes. As a leader, you probably need to process bigger chunks than your employees and smaller chunks than your manager. Ideally, your employees will learn that you don't want to hear all the details of their jobs, and you will learn the same about your manager.

It is especially useful to be able to chunk up and chunk down when you need to improve communication. When talking to someone using bigger chunks, you can ask the question, 'What, specifically?' to get more details. When talking to someone using smaller chunks, you can ask, 'What is the intention of this?' or 'What is this an example of?' to encourage larger chunks. When you think about it, senior managers are in their roles because of their ability to operate at all levels of the hierarchy. So the more flexible you can become the more earning potential is available to you.

You can also use this technique for overcoming boredom. Why do people get bored? Often because what they are doing does not excite them. They are bogged down in the details. If you have an outcome and you are not excited about it, ask yourself the question, 'This outcome for what purpose?', i.e. chunk up. Get a bigger perspective or the big picture. Having an outcome and not knowing the larger purpose can be demotivating.

This process can also be used for addressing overwhelm. This can happen if the chunk size is too large. Here you need to chunk down and be more specific or focus more on the details or be more realistic. After all, how do you eat an elephant? One bite at a time!

If you feel overwhelmed or do not know where to start when you think of your outcome; chunk down to be more specific and identify manageable tasks.

Lateral thinking using the Hierarchy of Ideas
Let's go back to thinking laterally or out of the box. We are often encouraged to think this way. This is not always easy to

do. It is if we use chunking. To think laterally, first chunk up, get some different ideas and only chunk down when you have a potential new solution. This is exactly what Einstein meant when he said problems could not be solved on the level they were created at. For example, imagine you live in a rural community. Traffic is becoming a real issue for your village and the district council wants to come up with some unique ideas for solving the problem. You are unlikely to solve this problem on the level of 'cars' because all cars in this context are an issue. However, if you chunk up to 'transportation', you can now ask the question 'what are different examples of transportation that could help us?' One example might be 'park and ride'. If that's feasible you can then chunk down to firm up the details.

Exercise 19: The chunking challenge

Step 1: Think of an issue which is holding your team back at the moment. (For example, your staff want flexi-time. This isn't possible)

Step 2: Use the 'chunking up' questions to chunk up to the next level of abstractness.

- What is this an example of?
- For what purpose?
- What is your intention?

(For example, flexi-time is an example of what? It's an example of a reward.)

Step 3: Ask yourself how this level gives you some new ideas. If necessary, chunk up another level. (For example, what alternative rewards could be more acceptable?)

Step 4: Start to chunk down only when you have a potential solution to explore further.

Pulling everything together

You may have felt yourself feeling a little 'tranced out' during this chapter. That's because I used a creative technique called 'inductive' teaching to get across these concepts. This approach is also known as 'discovery learning' because it helps the learner use more of their cognitive abilities to make connections between a range of ideas. Inductive learning works effectively with creative learners with very high motivation to 'have a go'. Most of our 'traditional' learning is taught deductively, i.e. you are given a topic and you chunk down into the detail. In this chapter I've deliberately given a number of alternative techniques for you to consider without drawing any strong conclusions or comparisons. The advantage of the inductive approach is that the learning just keeps on going way beyond the limitations of the written word.

So experiment with the different techniques and styles and find the one that works for you and your team. What is certain is that it is the team with the highest ability to create and differentiate itself that will get the best results. Good luck!

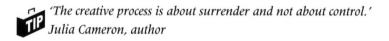 *'The creative process is about surrender and not about control.'*
Julia Cameron, author

6
Having Courageous
Conversations

///

'Appraisals and one-to-ones in my business are seen as a chore and a complete waste of time. The mere mention generates endless groans amongst staff and managers alike. Pointless hours are spent ticking boxes and having warm and fuzzy conversations with staff. I wish I could find a way to make them add real value to my team and for staff to welcome them as an opportunity.'

Regional Manager from a Household Name Charity

For how many of you do the words 'feedback', 'one-to-ones', 'supervision' and 'appraisals' generate a dull dread in the pit of the stomach? I've worked with many businesses in my career and this seems to be a key issue for the majority of them because people do not want to hear negative feedback and they certainly don't want to give it. It's easy to understand why people do not want to hear negative feedback. It doesn't feel good for a start because it is normally linked to criticism and what has gone wrong. Huge potential value and efficiencies for business is being left on the table whilst staff at all levels collude around the issue of poor performance. Alternatively, a 'courageous conversation' helps you and your staff to get to the next level faster because it helps you all to adjust your actions in real time rather than at some arbitrary measurement point called an 'appraisal'.

This chapter shows how feedback provided through 'courageous conversations' is the missing link to high-performing individuals and teams. Of course, feedback is about more than just a 'CC' – it is about holistic evaluation and not only what needs to be improved but also what was good about the performance. In this chapter you are going to particularly focus on developmental feedback given in the form of a 'CC' because, as leaders, this provides you with the greatest leverage for change.

Why do we fear being honest?

In our culture the fear of being honest often leads to the 'halo' effect or playing 'safe' with each other. The result is that over-complimentary feedback is given because we do not want to hurt the feelings of the recipient or we do not want to rock the boat. I often term this as 'bullshit' feedback! Often whole businesses collude with this system because it keeps everything running smoothly but not necessarily running well.

I was curious to find out why we behave in this way. I discovered an article called 'The Abilene Paradox' by Jerry B. Harvey which seemed to go a long way in explaining this from a social conformity perspective. It involves a common breakdown of group communication in which each member mistakenly believes that their own preferences run counter to the group's and, therefore, does not raise objections. Harvey argues that we say nothing or dress up negative feedback because of:

● **Action anxiety.** Giving honest feedback creates intense anxiety in the giver as they think about acting in accordance with what they know to be right. As a result they act in a manner incongruent with their beliefs.

- **Negative fantasies.** The giver builds up in their mind the negative consequences of speaking their truth until they are completely paralysed by the thought of it.

- **Fear of separation.** Probably the biggest reason for 'bullshit' feedback as the giver fears separation from the norm or the group if they take the risk of speaking out. We fear losing a friendship we value or losing the respect of our boss.

This begins to explain why a lack of authentic feedback is so prevalent in business today.

A club or a business?

I was asked to review the performance management systems within a public sector client. My review consisted of an audit of appraisal forms from the last round of reviews and follow up interviews. What soon became clear was the amount of collusion between staff. Poor performance was not judged honestly and staff were let off the hook too easily by their managers. There were two key reasons for this:

1. Line managers felt the HR system for dealing with poor performance was far too complex and favoured the person being given the feedback. They also described a lack of support at senior level to 'take things all the way to dismissal'. They used this as an excuse to not even 'try' to improve performance levels of staff.

2. They were concerned about the impact on their relationship with the individual which they feared would deteriorate making it even harder to get them to behave appropriately (reference the Abilene Paradox).

In addition, the majority of one-to-one sessions during the year were informal and reactive and the quality of the conversations and degree of challenge was questionable.

What is a 'courageous conversation'?

Courageous conversations are those difficult conversations every manager needs to have with staff when they aren't performing at an acceptable level. Extensive and expensive performance management systems can be useful but without courageous conversations the key to ensuring high performance from your employees is missing. However, the vast majority of managers are either unable or unwilling to have these conversations. This does not just affect the manager and the individual; it has a rippling effect, spreading disaffection amongst everyone else – particularly high-fliers who watch under-performance going unaddressed. The result can only be lower morale and higher turnover.

A CC can take on several different forms such as:

- **Day-to-day, informal, 'in the moment' conversations.** These are by far the best way to have a CC as it takes place immediately the incident occurs. For example, you've just heard a member of your team complaining to a colleague about another team member. This is not in line with the agreed behaviours of the team. You go straight up to them tell them about the poor behaviour you've noticed and how you'd like them to behave in future.

- **In one-to-one sessions.** Here you would use a CC to address a pattern of poor behaviour or performance issue, again being very specific about what you'd like the person to do differently in future.

- **In annual appraisal meetings.** Although a CC can take place in an appraisal meeting, this is the least preferred approach as any developmental feedback should have been given when the event happened and not stored up for a once or twice a year session. Though you might use the appraisal to plan a personal development solution to poor performance, such as training or coaching.

How do I know I need to have a courageous conversation?

Some questions to ask yourself:

- Is your team performing as well as it could?

- Are you getting the results that you want?

- How are the relationships within the team?

- How are your specific relationships with your team members and your boss?

Or you may have some far more obvious clues:

- You're angry at someone

- You're avoiding someone

- You're embarrassed about something

- You feel bad about something

- You're scared of about someone's reaction

- You're worried about the consequences of the conversation, and

- When you imagine the conversation, you feel uncomfortable

And the best clue of all: *You probably don't want to have the conversation*! This is a sure sign that your system is avoiding something. In a nutshell – you probably haven't had the CC yet because you're afraid of the outcome; that you'll lose a friendship or feel very uncomfortable.

Why should I have this courageous conversation?

Maybe a better question is what will happen if you don't? In the case study, the organisation was performing like a club – very polite, reactive and avoiding any difficult issues. If you want to develop a high-performing team then you need to encourage openness and honesty in the team and that begins with you. A team that lives with 'an elephant in the room' – i.e. they live with an issue that everyone knows about but no-one is courageous to bring out into the open – will never become a high-performing team. For example, this might be about the under-performance of one member of the team. Everyone covers up for them but no-one likes doing it. This kind of example often builds to a lack of respect for you as the leader for not dealing with the issue, especially by the best performers in your team.

Often the thoughts of having a CC are built up to be much worse in our heads than they are in reality. Remember what was covered in Chapter 2 about the power of our thoughts? If you think your CC will go badly then it probably will. If you're committed to constantly pushing back your boundaries – breaking through barriers to become a world-class team leader – then think positively and have the conversation. I'll show you how.

The effect on others

It's also amazing the effect it can have on the other person. Some people justify not having the conversation by saying, 'I'll just move on', or 'It's enough that I know about it', or 'It might upset them'. In my experience, having the conversation in your head isn't enough (unless they have died). It's in the speaking it to them that transformation occurs for both of you.

And another benefit: Imagine how fearless they might be once they've seen you set an example. Your courage can ripple out and change the world – well, at least your team. I've had people say: 'You know, after you called me, I started thinking. And I picked up the phone and called…'

Now I'm not guaranteeing you or they will like the results. However, in my experience, and in the experience of my clients, the outcome has almost always been positive in some way. Often, you find that staff are grateful for the feedback as they were not aware of the impact of their behaviour or actions on the rest of the team. We all have blind spots and often a CC will identify a blind spot for someone on your team. Imagine that you know something really important for someone and you choose not to tell them about it. That might have a really negative impact on their potential development. What right have you got not to tell them? Now that's an interesting perspective.

It's true you have a responsibility to speak with compassion, and to speak honestly. It's really important to hold in mind a positive intention for the other person at all times and to speak from the heart, not from anger or bitterness. This will increase your level of empathy with the other person and their situation. And, it's also true that no matter how compassionately or gently you share the truth, the other person may feel some pain. In my experience, however, it usually does more good than harm in the long run. It's important to note that it's very common to use 'It might upset them' as an excuse for wimping out of the CC.

Say it the way it is!

NLP helps us prepare for a CC. One of the things that you learn as a new NLP Practitioner is that it's important to 'say it the way that it is'. Also, to communicate with the person who can solve the problem. This is counter-intuitive in many business-es where people spend hours of wasted effort moaning about someone's performance to everyone except the person who can change the behaviour! Does that sound familiar to you?

You will learn a mindset to successfully address the problem and some alternative processes to prepare for tough and often uncomfortable conversations.

The mindset for a courageous conversation

You learned in Chapter 3 about the core principles of NLP. One of the most important elements to help us re-frame the whole challenge of feedback is: 'There is no failure, only feedback'.

In other words, there is only learning. I discussed this as well from the perspective of being at cause and taking responsibil-ity for your own development. If you truly embrace this then feedback becomes something to be welcomed and not some-thing to be feared as it is fundamental to you and your staff stepping up to the next level. I use this principle all the time with those I coach as it helps people to be less hard on them-selves about things that don't go to plan first time around.

There are other principles that also support our ability to give and receive feedback.

'Everyone has a different model of the world and their perception is their own truth.'

Whilst you may not agree with the feedback you have been given it is true for the giver in that situation. Each person's perception is unique to them and represents their own model of the world. That does not make it right or wrong it is just true for them. By accepting the feedback from someone you are ac-cepting that part of ourselves as they experience it. If, however, you receive similar feedback from many sources then it is very likely that there is something for you to consider.

'If you can spot it, you got it,' said NLP trainer Sue Knight at the NLP annual conference. In other words, what we recognise in others is true about ourselves. The characteristics in others that touch us emotionally are pointers toward those characteristics that we don't like in ourselves. You may notice that you dissociate from the characteristics that you don't like in others. Yet these are often 'blind spots' in us. To see something in others, you have to have that 'structure' in your thinking too, otherwise you would not recognise it. Interesting thought, isn't it?

Taking on these beliefs helps you to begin to change your own mindset around feedback and to begin to see it as something useful.

How to deliver a courageous conversation

Have you ever tried to give someone feedback only to have them get all angry and defensive? Or perhaps you have more experience with it the other way around, wanting to strangle the well-meaning boss who is giving you the feedback. Here are two NLP-based approaches to giving feedback using a CC.

The NLP feedback sandwich

Feedback is usually given like this:

> *Manager*: I really like the way you went after the new account and made the sale, but you really need to spend more time in the office cold calling...

The person receiving the feedback will always focus on the last statement. In addition, we are often not conscious that the word 'but' functions to negate what's been previously said. So typically the salesperson ends up muttering to themselves that no matter what improvements they make the boss just notices the negative so why even bother making the effort to improve sales.

The NLP feedback sandwich works like this, keeping eye contact and focus on the person at all times:

Step 1: Tell them the positive first, i.e. what they have done well recently. Example: 'I really like the way that you went after the new account and made the sale. You were very tenacious.'

Step 2: State the concerns (link Steps 1 and 2 with 'and', not 'but'). Example: 'And I have some concerns about the amount of time you spend in the office cold calling. What ideas do you have about improving this?'

Step 3: Finish with an overall positive statement like 'I really appreciate your efforts and your commitment to the sales team and your efforts to meet your sales target,' etc.

This is an approach that works well in the moment and is likely to make the receiver less defensive. Fast feedback is built into the daily routine, ideally at the moment that the event happens or at the end of a meeting or at the end of the day. The important thing is to say the feedback the way it is. Be as direct as possible – do not leave the opportunity for misinterpretation and give as many specific examples as you can. Vague feedback or hints in the hope that someone may get the point are meaningless.

It's important to focus on what the person should do differently and not on what they did wrong. As we learned earlier, the unconscious mind cannot process a negative. Remember 'don't think of a blue elephant!' To not think of a blue elephant you have to first think of a blue elephant. So if you focus on what you shouldn't do, you attract that exact thing to yourself.

An alternative NLP approach: Preparing a 'courage sheet'

You can devise your own 'courage sheet' to prepare for the conversation. Use this sheet to write down what you want to cover with the individual under each of the eight steps.

Step 1: Be specific about the issue to be discussed. For example, let's take the issue of a sales person struggling to meet their targets: 'I'm concerned that you are unlikely to meet your sales targets for this month.'

Step 2: Select a specific example that illustrates what you want them to change: 'I've observed that you do not spend anywhere near as long on the phone making cold calls as your colleagues do.'

Step 3: Describe how you feel about the situation: 'I'm feeling very frustrated about this as we've spoken about it before and I believe you have the potential to be an excellent sales person.'

Step 4: Give them the motivation to change: 'This is important not only for you to meet your targets but also because your results are dragging the whole team's results down.'.

Step 5: Check you haven't missed anything; 'Is there anything else I need to know about this situation?'

Step 6: Ask them what ideas they have to resolve the issue: 'What suggestions do you have to sort this out? What's stopped you from doing that already?'

Step 7: Check what you can do to help: 'How can I assist you to get your calls done? Do you need more training? Tell me how I can help. I really want to get this resolved as soon as possible.'

Step 8: Check their level of resolve to sort out the issue: 'On a scale of 1–10 (10 is high) how willing are you to sort this out?'

This method takes the most preparation and so is best suited for one-to-one's, personal development planning sessions at annual appraisal meetings and so on. It's a very helpful checklist for you to mentally rehearse in your mind and to visualise the conversation going well. It's starting to move you into much more of a coaching discussion.

///

Exercise 20: Having a courageous conversation

Go through the following questions and decide who you want to have a courageous conversation with, for what purpose and which process you will use. This will allow you to plan for the event. Remember to consider what it feels like to have the CC as well.

● The person I want to have a CC with is:

- This is the outcome I want to achieve by having this CC:

- This is the process (i.e. feedback sandwich or courage sheet) I have chosen and why:

- Record below what I learned from having the CC:

Coaching for success

'I never cease to be amazed at the power of the coaching process to draw out the skills or talents that were previously hidden within an individual, and which invariably find a way to solve a problem previously thought unsolvable.'

John Russell, Managing Director, Harley-Davidson Europe

The link between having a courageous conversation and improved performance is coaching. Coaching is an effective modern management technique for getting the best out of your team members. Between 20 and 40 per cent of Fortune 500 companies use executive coaches, according to the Hays Group, an international human resources consultancy.

What is coaching?

There are a lot of myths and misconceptions about coaching so let's look at a comparison between what coaching is and what it is not. See if this fits with your own idea of coaching.

Coaching is not about...	Coaching is about...
Telling someone what to do	Asking questions to draw the answers out of the coachee
Demonstrating your own expertise	A belief in the potential of your people to grow
Asking leading questions	Encouraging responsibility in the coachee
Forcing someone to do what you want them to do	Allowing the coachee to decide the best course of action
Letting the coachee off the hook	Holding the coachee to account
Training, mentoring or counselling	Finding ways to facilitate change in behaviour to create positive, long-term results

An NLP-based coaching model

Coaching sessions vary greatly in terms of their dynamics and what is covered so, in many ways, there is no such thing as a typical coaching session. However, here's an NLP-based model which has been developed and refined at the Change Corporation. It's called the Future/Present/Belief/Action

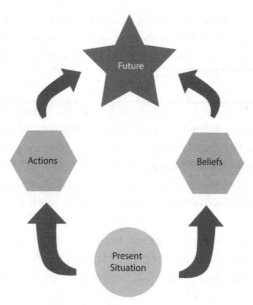

FPBA Coaching Model

or FPBA Model because it focuses not only on where the coachee is now in relation to their goals, but also what they believe it is possible for them to achieve. Many other coaching models do not include the 'Belief' stage. Without this stage, the risk is that a set of actions will be agreed, but if the coachee does not fundamentally believe that they can achieve them, their goals will not be actualised. Henry Ford said: 'If you think you can do a thing or think you can't do a thing, you're right.'

Here's the FPBA process in more detail:

Step 1: Identify the desired **Future** state, i.e. where does your coachee want to get to? Identify short-term and long-term goals, and the goal for the coaching session. Make sure they are all SMART (see Chapter 1).

Step 2: Identify the **Present** situation, i.e. what is happening right now? Where is your coachee in relation to their goals? Focus on the current situation – current challenges, performance and strategy.

Step 3: Identify what **Beliefs** your coachee has about themselves in relation to their goals. What are their empowering beliefs that will support them in this endeavour? What limiting beliefs will hold them back? (Refer back to changing limiting beliefs in Chapter 2). What can they do to change these limiting beliefs? How can you help with training, etc?

Step 4: What **Actions** do they sign up to undertake to move towards the future state? It's important that these actions come from your coachee so they are fully motivated to complete them.

Ask open questions and do not lead your coachee. This is about their empowerment and not being told what to do!

As a guideline, a coaching session will:

- Often have the coach talking for no more than 40 per cent of the time – ideally, much less!

- Have silences: if you ask a question, then the other person will need to think; don't be tempted to fill the silence with other questions

- Often need to be kept on track by the coach – your role is to hold the other person's agenda and ensure that you stay on track

- Result in clear and specific actions

- Address personal challenges and barriers to achievement to help the coachee understand and meet them

- Require rapport and trust to have an open dialogue

- Often follow a model such as the FPBA model, but not always

- Sometimes be short and involve you asking only one or two questions

- Always benefit from your full attention

- Involve you in active listening at all times and doing lots of reflecting back and summarising

Things to watch for in your coaching sessions

When you are coaching effectively you are watching for everything. You notice everything that is being communicated and look for a sense of congruence, an alignment between what is being said and all the non-verbal communication. (See Chapter 10, 'Influencing with Integrity' for further NLP models around rapport building.)

Below are some specific things to watch for in a coaching session:

- Is the coachee taking responsibility?

- Are they engaged with the coaching?

- Do they deliver on the agreed actions?

- Do they reflect on their performance?

- Do they take feedback on board?

If they don't, you will need to make this part of the coaching conversation and end the sessions if necessary. If the coaching commenced following a courageous conversation, you may need to consider moving into disciplinary grounds at this point.

Exercise 21: Holding a coaching session

Work with the person that you chose for your courageous conversation. Use the FPBA model to prepare for the session. Make a note of the results below and what you learned for next time:

● My outcome for the coaching session:

● How successful was the session against those results?

● What did I learn from holding the session?

● What would I do differently next time?

Pulling it all together

Let's reflect back on all the NLP tools that enable you to have a courageous conversation.

1. The most powerful feedback is given in the moment when the event occurred. It's easier for the person to remember and it's most readily understood by the unconscious mind if it's given immediately. Since all behaviour change occurs at the unconscious level, this means it has the very best chance of making an impact, especially when linked with one of the feedback models given.

2. In NLP, a particular mindset is emphasised that means over time staff begin to value feedback as a gift and not something to be afraid of. This mindset also encourages team members to be more open with each other.

3. In NLP, language is used with volition, structured in a specific way to get a particular result. The two approaches given here (the feedback sandwich and the courage sheet) enable feedback to be delivered in a thoughtful way that means the other person is likely to be less defensive and more open to influence (see more about NLP language patterns in Chapter 7).

4. Finally, use an NLP-based coaching model such as the FPBA to help your staff develop to the next level.

These combined NLP tools not only give you a process and the confidence to give feedback but also help you to develop your staff to give feedback to each other. Incorporating CCs and coaching into the culture of your team will fast-track everyone's performance. Your team members will follow your role model if you make CCs and coaching part of the way you do business in your team. By doing this you also give them permission to use CCs with each other and with you! You will notice that relationships in your team improve. They will become deeper and more meaningful as congruence, open-ness and honesty become the focus instead of avoidance. If you are a more senior leader and you can role model this across your business you will notice how managers and leaders become more confident and more resilient in challenging situations, being able to communicate in a more open and honest way and driving a high performance culture through-out the business.

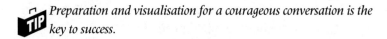 *Preparation and visualisation for a courageous conversation is the key to success.*

PART THREE

TRANSFORMING ORGANISATIONS WITH NLP

7
MANAGING CHANGE EFFECTIVELY

What is meant by change management? Simply, change management means changing people as well as things. The really interesting question is why do some change projects fail whilst others succeed? What can be learned from experience that can benefit you and where does NLP fit into all of this? These are the key questions that this chapter intends to answer.

Let's first explore what we mean by change management in the context of this book. There are three core areas in any change process: process, systems and people. In this chapter, we're going to explore the **people side** of change management. That means helping staff and customers through change. It is the processes, tools and techniques for pro-actively changing people's thinking and their behaviour in order to realise the anticipated benefits of the change programme.

According to Prosci's 2009 edition of *Best Practices in Change Management*, which surveyed 575 businesses across 65 countries, the greatest obstacles to successful change are:

- Ineffective change sponsorship from senior leaders
- Resistance to change from employees

- Insufficient resources and funding

- Middle management resistance

- Poor project management

- Ineffective communications

- An organisational culture that is resistant to change

Not managing the people side of change impacts on success and brings risk into a project. Focus on the people aspects can not only mitigate these business risks but in many cases avoid them altogether. Business leaders hold the key to making this happen yet they often do not appreciate their role in managing the people side of change until resistance is causing a major risk to the business benefits they have identified. As a 'people change' consultant, I'm often called in six months or so into the life-cycle of a project once these risks have finally been identified. However, it would have been much easier and cheaper to have avoided them in the first place. Business leaders often make two key mistakes: firstly, that changing thinking and behaviour is someone else's responsibility (normally HR), and secondly not responding fast enough when resistance does start to emerge.

So what are the greatest contributors to success? According to the Prosci *Best Practices* report there are five key factors:

1. Active and visible executive sponsorship

2. Frequent and open communication around the need for change

3. Structured change management approach

4. Dedicated resources and funding

5. Employee engagement and participation

I believe that engagement of middle managers and clarity about business benefits are also important. Prosci showed that projects with excellent focus on the people aspects of change were nearly six times as likely to realise the anticipated benefits than those teams with no or poor focus (95% to 16% respectively). Excellent people focus also correlated with staying on budget and to schedule.

In this chapter you'll discover how you can use NLP to build your leadership competency in all these critical success areas.

How NLP can help

There are many NLP tools that can help in this area. I've chosen the following as a powerful package where I've had amazing results:

- Setting clear outcomes and business benefits for the project
- Modelling the organisation itself to find out how it has managed change before.
- Using the language of success to influence others using:
  - firstly, the Meta Model – an exquisite model of questioning techniques
  - secondly, the Milton Model to manage resistance
- Building sponsorship and managing stakeholders using 'perceptual positions' or 'stepping into another's shoes'
- Using the 'Logical Levels of Change' framework to achieve sustainable results.

Let's explore each of these in turn.

Setting clear outcomes and business benefits for the project

'Through 2002, less than 25% of application projects will deliver hard, monetary benefits that exceed the cost of the implementation.' Gartner Research

Realising value is about ensuring that projects deliver the anticipated benefits claimed in the business case. The advantages of setting clear and measurable business benefits include having clear goals that can be communicated to staff, known costs and risks, and the return on investment is understood from the start. In contrast, vague business benefits lead to a lack of focus, wasted effort and money, frustrated and demotivated staff. This is not rocket science and yet, as the Gartner research shows, many businesses are not achieving this.

We learned in Chapter 1, 'Transforming Leaders with NLP', of the importance of having a personal leadership vision and setting clear goals to achieve that vision. Now we need to apply those same principles to formulating and communicating the strategic vision and articulating the associated benefits. We know that much staff resistance comes from not understanding why the change is happening and 'what's in it for me', or WIIFM. In particular, key concerns include 'will I have a job' and 'do I have the necessary skills and knowledge to survive in the new environment'. In fact, in some change programmes, the new terminology is about 'dis-benefits' where there is a benefit to the organisation but a dis-benefit to one or more groups of staff. A dis-benefit would include consequences such as job losses and redeployments.

One of the biggest mistakes made by change leaders is to define the benefits of the change only for senior executives, shareholders and customers, missing out middle and front-line staff. The dis-benefits to these levels of staff are often fudged or mis-communicated. In many, if not all, cases the real impact on the individual members of staff in the organisation is overlooked, or insufficiently recognised. The most effective programmes define the benefits on a number of levels – for the senior executives, shareholders, customers and for middle and front-line staff. These levels then drive the communications strategy and plan for the programme. For example, let's take a benefit of moving to a shared service centre for a regionalised business:

- Benefit to senior executives and shareholders is lower operating costs

- Benefit to customers is improved service levels

- Benefit to front-line staff and middle management is learning new skills and having a new career and promotions structure

Dis-benefit to front-line staff and middle management is job losses and redeployment to a new geographic location. If the change programme is 'sold' to staff only on the basis of lower costs and improved service levels there's likely to more resistance than if staff understand the full picture, i.e. both benefits and any potential dis-benefits.

Exercise 22: Realising business benefits

Pick an organisational change that either you are leading or you know about in your business.

Step 1 What's the vision for this change programme? Can you write it down in 50 words or less? Have a go:

Step 2 Define the benefits and any potential dis-benefits from the perspective of these audiences:

● Senior executives and shareholders:

● Customers:

● Middle managers and front-line staff:

///

How did you get on? Which did you find the most challenging? Was it the middle managers and front-line staff? This is the group normally paid least attention to at the start of a change project so it's not surprising how resistant they can become.

Using NLP to realise hard business benefits

The client is a London company providing Legal Document Management Services with 20 staff and a average turnover of £1.5m. The presenting problem was a lack of motivation in the sales team and the timing also happened to be March 2009 (the beginning of the worst recession ever to hit businesses in the UK). The target was to grow the business by 33%, in spite of the recession. An NLP-based coaching and training programme with the sales team and directors was designed as follows:

1. Profile sales staff and directors

2. Provide Meta Programme and MBTI report for the board and sales team and explain the implications to them as leaders of the business

3. Each member of the sales team and board to attend a 4-day NLP Business Diploma

4. One-to-one coaching and follow-on training days provided

The focus of the work was to change inflexible behaviours and limiting beliefs. Staff now recognise that there is no failure, there's just results. If the results aren't what they want, they'll keep modifying their behaviours until they find the model that works.

The results are impressive:

● New client acquisitions up by 200%

● New business meetings up from an average of 16 per month to an average of 40

'The original goal was to increase the average monthly sales turnover from £18,000 to £24,000. After only 10 months into the project the average turnover has already increased to £36,000 per month and is still rising. The return on investment was two months.' David Key, Managing Director, Auspicium.

Modelling the organisation on itself

In Chapter 3 you learned how to model world-class performance. You are now going to use that process to discover how
ready an organisation is to change. The purpose of this modelling is to learn how an organisation has managed past change
initiatives and how well it is geared up to deliver successful
change now. In other words, you can use this process at the
beginning of a change programme to gather information from
key stakeholders to understand the early actions required to
manage change risk and to lay the necessary foundations for a
successful change programme.

Exercise 23: How ready is your business for change?

Use the following Change Readiness Assessment to measure a
change process that is underway or about to start in your business.

Change Readiness Assessment
Scoring: 1 = inadequate 2 = adequate 3 =good 4 = exceptional

	Change Benefits	**Score**
1	There is an industry standard business case for this change programme	
2	Business benefits have been clearly defined and processes are in place to measure their delivery	
3	There is a compelling case for change which has been understood and believed by all levels of staff	
	Sub-total score:	
	Change Leadership	
4	The change programme has an executive sponsor who has the necessary authority to authorise and fund the change	
5	The sponsor is willing to champion the change and manage resistance from other managers and staff	

(Continued)

6	The sponsor is willing to demonstrate their personal commitment to the change through their actions and behaviours	
	Sub-total score:	
	Change Vision	
7	Staff understand what the change will mean for the business	
8	Staff understand 'what's in it for me'	
9	Line managers take the time to explain the change process to their staff	
	Sub-total score:	
	Change Approach	
10	A structured change management approach is being applied to this project	
11	Anticipated areas of resistance have been identified and strategies to overcome them have been developed	
12	Adequate change management resources have been appointed and trained in the approach	
	Sub-total score:	
	Change Commitment	
13	Staff believe this change will succeed	
14	Staff want this change to succeed	
15	Commitment is being built through good communication rather than forced	
	Sub-total score:	
	Change Capability	
16	Managers have the change skills necessary for this change process	
17	Staff are being trained to develop new attitudes, skills and knowledge (ASKs)	
18	HR policies reward new ASKs	
	Sub-total score:	

(Continued)

	Culture Change	
19	The new values of the business are clear and staff buy into them	
20	The existing culture is aligned to the new direction of the business or is being changed to align	
21	Leaders model the new values and behaviours	
	Sub-total score:	
	Change History	
22	This business has a reputation for completing change projects on time and realising benefits	
23	This business has built staff levels of commitment well in the past	
24	Linked projects have been well coordinated	
	Sub-total score:	
	Total score:	

Review your summary scores. Which areas have strong results and will support your change project and which areas present a risk to the project and require attention? Make a note of them below:

Let's now explore how to use NLP to build commitment and sponsorship for your project.

Using the language of success

The 'L' in NLP stands for linguistic and there are two powerful models of language that we are going to apply to the area of managing change. The first is the Meta Model – an exquisite model of questioning techniques. The second is the Milton Model – an equally exquisite model to engage with staff, build support and manage resistance.

Jeffrey M. Hiatt and Timothy J. Creasey, authors of *Change Management, The People Side of Change*, said that the natural and normal reaction to change is resistance. Each individual member of staff has a threshold for how much change they can absorb based on:

- Their personal history
- Current events in their life
- Current changes at work
- How much other change is going on

This will impact on how far they go into denial at the start of a change process and the level of resistance they will demonstrate. As a change leader, you therefore need to expect resistance and plan for it. The way you use your language in your communications planning and delivery is a critical success factor.

The Meta Model

Have you ever been chatting to someone about some aspect of your change programme and you find yourself wondering what on earth they are talking about? There seems to be some important information missing from their language or they are making massive assumptions. For example, they might say to you, 'It's a bad idea to implement this change in the business.' You might be left wondering, 'who says'. Or they might say to you, 'Every time we implement a change we make a mess of it.' You might well be left questioning 'every time'. People distort, generalise and delete their use of language all the time. This can be a particular challenge when implementing change as staff constantly mind-read what's going on, attach meanings to things that are not true and delete information that they do not want to hear.

Hiatt and Creasey said that: 'Change leaders must be conscious of both a sender's message and a receiver's interpretation.'

Change leaders often make the common mistake that their staff attach the expected meaning to their communication. They believe that because something has been communicated it has been understood. This very often is simply not the case. The Meta Model enables us to check and challenge what staff say by using a series of powerful questioning techniques. We are going to practise the Meta Model questions in the context of a change process – though it is a model that can be used in any communication interaction.

The Meta Model was NLP's first language model. It was modelled and then further developed by Bandler and Grinder from the work of Fritz Perls and Virginia Satir. The Meta Model's patterns were designed for the express purpose of challenging the limitations in the mental maps of others. Grinder said that the Meta Model pattern consisted of two components – the identification of the pattern and the challenge question/s designed to help that individual expand his or her map of possibilities. Put simply, the Meta Model is designed to recover information and new choices that the receiver has not yet noticed because of the way that they experience the world. For example, a staff member who believes their job to be at risk is likely to filter any communication through a mental map which is anxious, suspicious and fearful. We can use the Meta Model questions to help them notice other more positive possibilities.

The patterns

Here are the major patterns put into the context of a change programme. The table below shows the pattern and its 'formal' name, the impact it has, the challenge question to expand awareness of the receiver and the impact that we intend it to have on them.

Language pattern	Impact	Challenge question	Impact
Distortions			
I know you don't want to tell us what's really going on (Mind reads)	Claims to know how someone else is feeling or their internal state	*How do you know that?*	Challenges the statement and recovers the source of information
This change is bad for our team (Lost performative)	The person making the judgement is left out	*Who says it's bad or how do you know it's bad?*	Recovers the source of that belief which can then be challenged
The views of the leadership team really make me angry (Cause and effect)	Where cause is wrongly put outside of self and blamed on others	*How do the views of the leadership team cause you to choose to be angry?*	Recovers personal choice
This change in process means I'll lose my job (Complex equivalence)	Where two experiences are seen as synonymous	*How does this change in process mean that you'll lose your job?*	Recovers the source of that belief which can then be challenged
Generalisations			
We never engage with our staff (Universal quantifiers)	Generalises the whole experience	*Never?*	Recovers a counter example that helps the person change their views

(Continued)

Language pattern	Impact	Challenge question	Impact
Generalisations (*continued*)			
We should/have to leave things just as they are (Modal operator of necessity)	Turns the sentence into a necessity	*What would happen if we didn't? Or What would happen if we did?*	Encourages consideration of alternative outcomes
Deletions			
There's no communication here (Nominalisation)	Freezes a verb into a noun so it becomes stuck	*Who's not communicating what to whom?*	Turns the statement back into a process and the possibility of recovering the deletion
They don't listen to us (Lack of a referential index)	Makes a statement without specifying who made it	*Who specifically doesn't listen?*	Recovers the deletion
This new idea is too expensive (Comparative deletion)	Comparison made & not specified against what or whom	*Compared to what?*	Recovers the source of the comparison that can then be challenged
I am uncomfortable (Unspecified verb)	Leaves out the critical data	*How specifically are you uncomfortable?*	Recovers the missing data that can then be challenged

There are some principles that are important to use with this model as it can be experienced as very direct by the receiver. First of all, it's important to have a good relationship or rapport with the person (or team) making these comments. The receiver will be much more open to your questions if this is in place. Secondly, you can soften your approach by starting with 'I'm wondering…' or 'I'm curious…' or 'that's interesting…' For example, the last challenge question would then become 'That's interesting. How specifically are you uncomfortable?'

Exercise 24: Putting the Meta Model into practice

Step 1: For the next week, pay attention to the language used by your staff. You might find it easier to focus on one pattern at a time. For example, pay attention to the mind-reads first.

Step 2: When you hear the pattern, use a challenge question in response. Make sure you are in rapport and that you use a softening frame as well.

Step 3: Make a note of the results that you get below:

The Meta Model is like a secret weapon for any change manager. You can use it with laser-beam focus and purpose to challenge what someone is saying – it gets to the spot fast and can really help your staff to think differently about a situation.

The Milton Model

The other language model we are going to explore is the Milton Model, named after Milton Erickson whom Bandler and Grinder modelled. This became the third major NLP model (the second was Representational Systems that we will explore in

Chapter 10). They noticed that Erickson's use of language bore a relationship to the Meta Model in that he seemed to be using similar patterns but in an inverse way. Tosey and Mathison described that 'while the emphasis of the Meta Model was on recovering deleted material…Erickson would introduce deletions purposefully'.

Erickson used language in a way that managed the potential resistance of his clients. He used words in an artfully vague fashion so his clients could fit their mental maps into what he was saying. That got Erickson the agreement from his client that he needed to be able to get the best results for them. Clearly this has ethical implications, but Erickson used these techniques as a means to elicit and facilitate a client's positive change and not to impose his own will. It is important to bear this in mind when using these tools in the business environment. And of course, all communication is designed to influence another. As my NLP trainer taught me: 'We cannot not communicate even when we say nothing!'

The patterns

Here are the major patterns put into the context of a change situation. The difference is that this time we use these patterns ourselves to manage any potential resistance levels of our staff and build levels of motivation and engagement. The important point to bear in mind is that these patterns only have to be plausible, not necessarily true!

Language pattern	Impact	Result
I know that you're going to be surprised by the new skills you will learn from this change process (Mind reads)	Claims to know the benefits that someone else will get from the experience of change	Staff agree with the statement and feel more positive about what is to come

(Continued)

Language pattern	Impact	Result
It's easy to make these changes (Lost performative)	The person making the judgement is left out	You can make a sweeping judgement without having to own it yourself – offsets potential resistance
If you decide to get involved in the focus groups then you will be able to influence what happens next (Cause and effect)	Implies that there is a direct relationship between attending the focus group and having influence. Whilst this is plausible it may not be the actual case	Makes the focus groups appear to be more attractive to encourage staff to attend
Coming to this meeting means you'll be able to understand about the change process easily (Complex equivalence)	Two experiences are seen as synonymous. Whilst this is plausible it may not be the actual case	This example is used to encourage staff to believe they will learn quickly. It builds their confidence
We always ask our staff what they think of our ideas (Universal quantifiers)	Generalises the whole experience	Implies widespread consultation to build motivation

(Continued)

Language pattern	Impact	Result
We have to change or lose market share (modal operator of necessity)	Turns the sentence into a necessity	Makes the change sound really important and necessary
A decision will be made soon (Nominalisation)	Freezes a verb into a noun so it becomes stuck	Offsets any resistance and builds expectations without saying who will be making the decision and by when
Many people are enthusiastic about this change (Lack of a referential index)	A statement in which it is not clear who specifically the statement refers to	Implies lots of support without having to specify exactly how much
This new process is much better (Comparative deletion)	Where a comparison is made and it is not specified against what or whom the comparison was made	Implies a positive result without having to specify what it is being compared to
I am satisfied (Unspecified verb)	Leaves out the critical data	Implies a good result without having to be too specific
You know this makes sense, don't you? (Tag question)	A closed question added to the end of a statement	Encourages the receiver to agree with you

(Continued)

Language pattern	Impact	Result
As you sit there, listening to me, thinking about the change programme, wondering what it will mean for you, I know that you will find the whole experience useful (Pacing current experience)	Undeniably describing the client's internal or external experience	By creating a creating a series of internal 'yes's' you can add something at the end that you want the person to agree to so they are more likely to agree with you
Do you want to try out this new process today or tomorrow? (Double binds)	Where an illusion of choice is created but no matter which choice is taken the outcome is the same	Again is used to manage any potential resistance as the receiver still believes they are in control of the result
Do you realise that this is something you can do easily? (Conversational postulate)	A closed question, which creates the Internal Representation of something you want the client to do. It allows the client to choose to respond or not and avoids authoritarianism.	Builds confidence and motivation

(Continued)

Language pattern	Impact	Result
I know that you can volunteer to take part in the trial (Embedded command)	Directives embedded within the sentence which directs a person to do something	This delivers a double message – one to the conscious mind and the instruction to the unconscious mind

As with the Meta Model, it's important to have a good relationship or rapport with the person (or team) to which you are making these comments. Again the receiver will be much more open to your statements if this is in place. Use the patterns to gain agreement in meetings and manage potential resistance levels around change. Remember the beauty of the Milton Model is that it is artfully vague so everyone can fit their own mental maps inside it. You might wonder what place this has in business, yet if you listen to the conversations going on all around you, you will start to notice that ambiguous language is used all the time with great effect.

Exercise 25: Putting the Milton Model into practice

Step 1: For the next week, use the patterns with your staff. As before, you might find it easier to focus on one pattern at a time. For example, pay attention to using mind reads first.

Step 2: Notice the impact your statement has on the receiver.

Step 3: Make a note of the results that you get below:

The Milton Model is another secret weapon for any change manager. This time it's a tool to build staff engagement. Help your staff to become more positive and motivated about the journey and encourage them to get involved.

Building sponsorship and managing stakeholders

In this section you will learn how to manage challenging situations using an NLP tool called 'perceptual positions'. When I use this tool with business teams I call it 'Stepping into Another's Shoes' as it's easier for the groups to understand. One of the core principles of NLP, covered in Chapter 2, is that 'the person with the most flexibility will achieve the most'. How do you become more flexible? Well, those people who are able to experience a situation from many different perspectives are likely to have the mental agility to get the best outcome. This flexibility and agility is invaluable in a change management scenario in order to influence key stakeholders. Imagine how useful it would be if you could use this model to create awareness and engagement amongst staff and build sponsorship from the change leadership.

Essentially, the purpose of the model is to examine an existing scenario from a number of different perspectives. It is very useful for exploring change scenarios where resistance and blockages are preventing a project from moving ahead at the required pace.

How it works it that you take a situation with another individual or a group and explore that situation from three different perspectives as follows:

1. **First position.** This is your own Perceptual Position as you experience the situation. In NLP, we call this a fully associated position. That is, you are fully in it and living it as if it is happening right now. In this position you are fully able to appreciate what is important to you personally about the scenario.

2. **Second position.** This is the Perceptual Position of an 'other'. By putting yourself in second position you are able to understand more about where the other person or group is coming from, and what their model of world would need to be in order for them to behave in the way that they are. You experience the situation as if you were them. You do this by imagining what it is like to experience the world as they do. Of course, you can never exactly do this but it's amazing to give it a go. This is the one time when mind reads are especially useful!

3. **Third or observer position.** This is the 'helicopter view' – the objective position. This is the ability to stand back from the emotion of the scenario as if you are the detached observer. You ask yourself what can be learned from the behaviour of both parties.

In positions 1 and 2, ask yourself the following set of questions:

- What's going on? (i.e. as the other person when in position 2)
- How are you behaving?
- How are you feeling?
- What do you believe about the situation?
- What's important to you?
- What do you want to happen?
- What is there for you to learn from this position?

In position 3, ask yourself the following set of questions:

- What's going on?
- How are they each behaving?
- How are they each feeling?

- What beliefs do they each appear to be using?

- What's important to each of them?

- What do they want to happen?

- What is there for you to learn from this position?

Finally, come back into yourself, bringing your new learnings and perceptions with you. Ask yourself how the situation is different now. What new strategies can you develop to build relationships and get the other person or team on side?

///

Exercise 26: Putting yourself into someone else's shoes

Take a current situation where an individual or team is being re-sistant to change or where you require stronger sponsorship from a change leader. Take yourself through the exercise and make a note below of the new insights and actions that you can implement as a result:

///

Where and when can you use this approach?

This works well in face-to-face situations (and we can learn to do this in real time while we are in conversation) and it is just as relevant in other forms of communication. For example, we can apply this thinking to prepare for telephone calls, emails and presentations in a way that creates the outcome that we really want for our change programme. It's a tool that can be used in any business situation as the following case study demonstrates.

Stepping into a sponsor's shoes

A manager learned about 'stepping into another's shoes' and now uses the technique to prepare for his meetings with a key female client. He discovered from 1st position that he has a very logical approach to his work. He needs her support as the main client sponsor and buyer yet he wasn't connecting very well with her at all. Using this exercise, he put himself into her shoes and realised that she was more focused on feeling good about their relationship and building rapport than he was. Next time they met he experimented with a more 'emotional' approach with her. He spent time describing the history of his organisation and the ethics of the business rather than jumping straight to the specifics. This more supportive style built stronger empathy with the client. The relationship is now much stronger and the deal is progressing well.

Using the 'Logical Levels of Change' to achieve sustainable results

Finally, let's explore one of the greatest challenges to any change programme – how to ensure that the changes last. Robert Dilt's 'Logical Levels of Change' framework is very useful in exploring why change doesn't last and what to do about it. This model was originally published in *Changing Belief Systems with NLP* (Dilt, 1990).

The model consists of six hierarchical levels. The key principle is that each level contains content and information from the level below it and that a higher order change will necessarily affect the contents of the lower levels. However, though lower levels may influence higher levels they alone will not change them. Perhaps a better description would be 'levels of

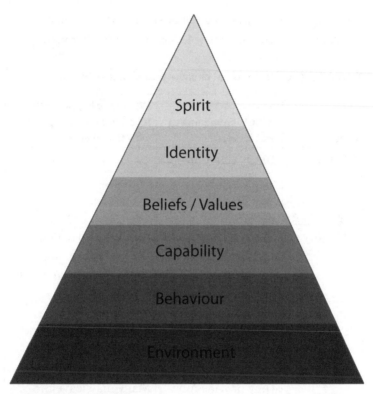

Logical Levels of Change

intervention'. For example, many change programmes fail because a change at a lower level of the hierarchy – say at the level of environment or behaviour or capability – is expected to be long term. However, if there is no alignment to the values or beliefs of those involved, the change process is likely to stall. That is why the whole process of the people side of change and building engagement strategies is so important. I've been involved in many 'sheep dip' training programmes before I got into NLP and was disappointed when they didn't create the long-term change required by the organisation. Now I understand the reasons why. If those being trained do not understand the compelling reasons for the change and do not see the changes as important they are likely to slip back into old behaviours. This chart shows where potential issues may occur in a change programme if the levels are not in alignment.

Translating 'logical levels of change' into business terms

Level	What's happening at that level?	What may happen if the levels are not in alignment with the level above
6 Spirit	This is about links to wider global systems and social responsibility	
5 Identity	The vision, mission and purpose of the business	Lack of connection. Seen as selfish, independent, isolated in the business world
4 Beliefs/ Values	Why people choose to do things. The rules and attitudes of the business. They provide motivation, permission, what's important and how people are evaluated	Conflicting priorities and values. Staff are conflicted about what is most important. Many may leave the business.
3 Capability	How they do it. For example, the knowledge, skills and abilities needed to do the work. Includes many training programmes	I can but don't want to... staff are de-motivated, bored with a lack of drive. Staff know what needs to change but they don't understand why they should. They revert to old ways.

(Continued)

Level	What's happening at that level?	What may happen if the levels are not in alignment with the level above
2 Behaviour	What people do – their actions/ reactions	Here staff are told to perform in a different way (behaviour) without receiving the necessary training (capability/ strategy). Unfortunately, this happens far too often. When money becomes tight, the first thing cut is the training budget! Again the change will most likely not be long-lasting. The risk is random behaviours, habits. Staff repeating old behaviours even if they don't work.
1 Environment	Where and when people do things. The environment they work in.	If there is a change to the physical layout of the office it will only be seen to be beneficial if it is understood to be part of the delivery of the wider change programme. If this doesn't happen the impact will be a hollow environment. Nothing gets done. Staff become de-motivated. Risk is that they don't follow the rules

Exercise 27: Using logical levels in your change programme

When designing your own change management intervention, the following set of questions may help to set a context to achieve long-term change:

- What is the ultimate mission of this business and what link to wider global systems does it want to achieve?

- What vision and purpose will support that?

- What core values and beliefs support this mission?

- What capabilities support each of these core values and beliefs?

- What behaviours support each capability?

- What environment supports these behaviours?

Staying at No. 1

The top bank in the Netherlands had invested in an expensive sales training programme but its results didn't change. The training had provided both knowledge and skills training (i.e. levels 2 and 3 on the model). Staff knew what to do. Yet, their attitude towards sales was still not the right one. The missing link was that the account managers, advisors and sales representatives didn't change their attitudes and beliefs towards sales and acquisition (level 4 on the model). We were tasked to come up with a 2-day programme that changed their mindset towards sales.

We used the NLP Communication model, the NLP frames: Cause and effect, perception = projection, responsibility for change and the pre-supposition that anything less than 100% = sabotage. We also explained the logical levels of change and aligned team values. Finally, we introduced the feedback sandwich for giving and receiving feedback. This enabled all delegates to maximise their learning in the most constructive way.

The 2-day programme was a mix of indoor and outdoor activities to challenge the delegates' beliefs about sales possibilities. Then we provided training on the job to practise cold calling. Two months later there was a follow-up day in which the participants had to present their results since the first training.

We have trained over 35 banks. This time, all the trained banks did improve their sales performance and the bank is still the number 1 in Holland.

From: Eelco Wisman, Managing Director of OUTWISE Performance Improvement, Holland

Pulling it all together

Often business leaders are frustrated when change programmes do not deliver the benefits that were promised at the start. NLP gives us a range of tools that can help with the 'people side of change' by building engagement and commitment. The biggest learning for change leaders is that compliance methods in change programmes don't work or they work well only in the very short term. If you want true sponsorship, engagement and commitment from leaders and staff you have to invest time and energy into helping them:

- Understand the compelling case for change

- Be clear about the business benefits and WIIFM

- Identify the readiness and the ability of the business to deal with the changes

- Influence others by using your communications with purpose and volition

- Resolve challenging situations and relationships

- Align changes with their values and beliefs and get them to feel part of the identity of the business.

That's when the real magic of change starts!

There is always a choice to be made in change management – compliance vs commitment. Compliance can work in the short term but only commitment builds sustainable change.

8

CHANGING THE RULES
OF THE GAME

//

Changing corporate culture is heavy-duty stuff. I've called this chapter 'Changing the Rules of the Game' (ROTG) because that's exactly what needs to be done. This isn't the sort of challenge that you take on because it's the 'in thing' to do. You do it because you have to in an attempt to survive or, if you're smart enough, you do it before you have to. However, most businesses do not have the foresight to change their culture before the market forces them to – remember Marks and Spencer? Some start then don't have enough determination to carry things through, whilst others tinker around the edges and wonder why they don't get the results that they expected.

We are going to explore how NLP can help rewrite the ROTG and assist to you achieve dramatic culture shifts in a short space of time. Here are the NLP concepts we'll use for this:

- Pattern break

- Strategies

What are the 'rules of the game'?

Essentially these are the unconscious rules of the organisation. They're what everyone learns when they join yet are never taught. They're everything that operates behind the scenes and drives behaviour in the business. These are not normally the conscious mission statements, values and behaviours rewarded at annual appraisal time. Instead, they are what everyone understands to be the way that things really get done (or not). It's rather like an iceberg. The visible tip represents the areas of culture that we can see in the physical sense. These 'visible' elements include things such as policies and procedures, reward practices and performance measures, structure, environment, leadership actions, corporate plan, organisation mission statement, vision and values, behaviours and so on. These are all important shapers of culture.

However, none of the visible elements can ever make real sense without an understanding of the drivers behind them; and these are hidden below the water level of the iceberg or on the invisible side. These invisible elements are the underlying causes of what manifests on the visible side. So, when thinking about culture, the below sea level of the iceberg will include things such as 'real' values and beliefs, climate, symbols of culture and norms. For example, a new behaviour identified at visible level might be for staff to take more risks. However, if at an invisible level the leadership blames staff for the mistakes that are made, that is unlikely to happen. There is often a mismatch between what people are told to do and the actions of their leaders or the environment in which they work.

Here are a couple of fascinating examples. One of my clients, a major UK utility company, wanted to change culture and break down hierarchies, yet all the senior managers had offices on what the staff jokingly described as 'mahogany row'. This was because of the massive mahogany desks that all the offices on 'mahogony row' contained. Of course, no-one else in the organisation had these desks. Another time I was working on a services base which wanted to break down the divide between civilian and service personnel. One key factor was to improve communication between both groups yet the Base Commander used to arrive through the back door each morning so he didn't risk having to speak to anyone.

'Be the change you want to see in the world.'

Mahatma Ghandi

In business this should be translated for the leadership as 'demonstrate the changes you want to see in your business'. In this way, culture can either enable and reinforce strategy or undermine its direction and threaten the implementation of change initiatives.

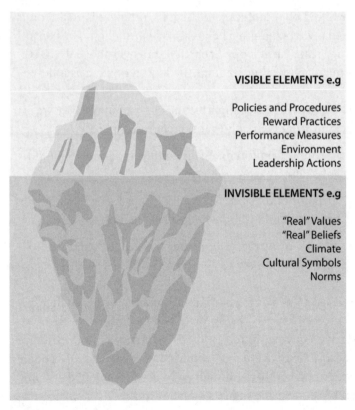

VISIBLE ELEMENTS e.g

Policies and Procedures
Reward Practices
Performance Measures
Environment
Leadership Actions

INVISIBLE ELEMENTS e.g

"Real" Values
"Real" Beliefs
Climate
Cultural Symbols
Norms

Iceberg

The ROTG represent the whole area beneath the water level or – as I call it – your business 'immune' system. Unless you are able to overwhelm its offences it will launch a counter-offensive which often wins. That's why attempts at incremental change rarely work in culture change. If you go too slow the existing bureaucracy and resistance to change will cancel out all your efforts. You cannot change culture according to the old rules.

Moving an oil tanker

I worked on a project some years ago now where attempts at changing engrained behaviours kept stalling. The consultancy team carried out research to uncover the real 'ROTG'. It made interesting reading. The key rules were as follows:

- We say we want simplicity and clarity, but the way we act (and what we really want) creates complexity

- We are uncomfortable with conflict, and prefer comfortable failure to uncomfortable success

- At point of tension, we would rather focus on changing process than dealing with the people issues

- A spirit of wanting to please, leading to 'blind' compliance with process

These ROTG were undermining many of the change initiatives that were being delivered at surface level. Leaders were giving up too easily at the first point of resistance because they were not comfortable dealing with people issues and conflict and they were used to quietly sweeping failures under the organisational carpet.

We concluded that most of the key observations were not about deficiencies in the processes, but about the way people led, communicated and discharged their responsibilities. None of the process improvements required would deliver success until these other issues had been dealt with.

This feedback came as a shock to the management team who had no idea how endemic these issues had become. It served as a shock tactic to get them to start thinking differently about the culture challenge ahead.

Exercise 28: What are the rules of your game?

This is best completed by carrying out interviews and focus groups with key stakeholders in your business. Depending upon your position, you may prefer to delegate this to someone else or even a consultant from outside the business. In my experience, staff are normally more open to those who they know will communicate their views anonymously. It is important to hold one-to-one interviews with senior stakeholders. Focus groups are useful for front-line staff and groups of customers.

Use these suggested questions below to help you uncover your organisation's immune system. Add more of your own that are specific to your environment:

- What's most important to the leaders of this business?
- How are decisions made?
- How far do the leaders of this business 'walk the talk', i.e. do they adopt the behaviours they expect others to adopt?
- What are the key symbols in this business and what do they tell us about what is really going on (e.g. personal car-parking spaces, segregated restaurants, after work socialising, etc.)?

- What are the underlying patterns of behaviour in this business?
- What are the key formal and informal communication channels?
- What's the appetite for risk?
- What's the one thing that staff complain about most? What does this tell us about the immune system?

How was that? Did you discover anything interesting? My guess is that you did. You may well be able to use the information you uncovered in the next section.

Using a pattern break to 'disarm' the old culture

Now you have a greater level of awareness of the challenge that lies ahead, let's look at how to get started in making a culture change programme work. In NLP, the concept of the 'pattern break' is a useful one here. By 'pattern break', I mean a series of abrupt interruptions that permanently break a habit or state. In the business context this can be translated to mean that something has to happen to shatter the status quo and let people know, especially supporters of the existing culture, that you are serious about the change. Incremental change is less likely to work in this instance. Take an action (or actions) that makes people sit up and listen. Make sure your opening actions leave no doubt that the old culture is incompatible with what is to come. If this worries you, then maybe a major culture change is not for you or your business at this time as it requires focus, radical action and risk. Yet the rewards of a culture which reinforces business strategy are potentially enormous.

Examples of a pattern break in this context include (this is not an exhaustive list):

- Revamp the reward system
- Reduce the levels of hierarchy

- Radical reorganisation

- Outsource non-vital functions

- Lose staff who are not performing

- Abolish elitist benefits for senior staff

- Adopt flexible working methods, e.g. desk sharing

You will find that the pattern break does not have to be major in size – throwing out the mahogany desks would have as much impact as many others on the list. Of course, the pattern break you choose should align with the changes you wish to achieve. For example, outsourcing or flexible working methods may go along with major budget cuts. A pattern break like this is required because the current culture has a very strong immune system. Unless you can overwhelm it quickly and weaken it somehow, it is likely to launch a counter-offensive and it usually wins. Of course, a heavily unionised environment will play a part here too. The benefits of the new culture must be clear and be seen to outweigh the old culture. If at all possible, get the union onside before launching any major change programme.

Exercise 29: What's your pattern break?

From the results of the interviews and meetings you held earlier (Exercise 25) to identify the features of the immune system of your business, consider what actions would produce the effects of a 'pattern break' in your business:

Disarming the 'club'

(Back to the case study we explored in Chapter 6.) We wanted to demonstrate to staff that the 'club' culture was no longer acceptable. Before the next round of appraisals was due, the senior management team introduced some new measures to create a pattern break into the business. Firstly, a panel was established to moderate the appraisal results across different teams. Any manager could be called to the panel to justify their scores. Secondly, line managers had to justify their assessments with their own managers before any appraisals went to moderation. Thirdly, a new performance management system was put into place across the business with more interim reviews during the year. This certainly demonstrated to managers that the organisation was serious about the change process. Finally, all managers received training in how to set objectives for staff and deliver a 'quality conversation'.

Once your opening moves have turned heads and shown conviction, it's time to explore what's the best strategy to use to introduce long-term culture change in your business.

A culture change strategy

The 'P' in NLP stands for programming. This is the way that you do things or your strategies for success. If you have an area of your life where you are not yet getting the results that you want, you can be sure that it's because of the strategy that you are running in that area. It's the same in business. Let's look at the subject of strategies in the context of NLP and then apply it to culture change. And, of course, strategies apply to everything that you do so what you learn here will have a broader application in your business. For example, if the way you communicate in your business is not working the way you want it to, how do you need to change your strategy for communicating that will get you better results?

In NLP terms, a strategy is a sequence of thoughts and behaviours that lead to a specific result. You will have learned strategies that either work for you or against you. NLP helps you to unravel step by step the strategies that do not work well so you can change them. The saying, 'If you always do what you've always done you always get what you've always got' is very relevant here. If something is not working in your life do something different! It's the same principle for business.

The TOTE

The TOTE is the fundamental model used in NLP strategies. I notice that a lot of my NLP students find the concept of the TOTE pretty mind-boggling so I'm going to explain it here as simply as possible.

The TOTE model was developed in 1960 (published in *Plans and the Structure of Behaviour*) by psychologists Eugene Galanter, Karl Pribham and George Armitage Miller to describe and explain human behaviour. The acronym TOTE stands for:

- **Test** – Here we set or access the criteria for the *desired state*.
- **Operate** – Here we access or gather the data
- **2nd Test** – We compare or evaluate the data in respect to the criteria
- **Exit** – We select or prioritise the data and exit if we have a match

Everything anyone does involves a TOTE. Sue Knight said that:

> 'The principle is that our behaviour is driven by an out-come (desired state) and we recognise when we have achieved that outcome by a set of evidence criteria... We are constantly comparing our present state to our desired state to find out if they match. When they do match we have reached the exit point or our outcome. If the present state does not match our desired state we have to do another operation to discover if that makes a difference.'

We are all running TOTEs constantly and comparing where we are to where we want to be and taking action to get ourselves closer to the exit point. The TOTE is a feedback loop. Key skills to get through the TOTE are: sensitivity to what is happening around you, a willingness to learn from feedback, and the flexibility to do something different when what you are doing is not working.

Here is an example. Recently, I wanted to buy a new telephone that I could use to receive my emails on the move.

- 1st Test: I worked out a list of my criteria for what gadgets I wanted on my new phone
- Operate: I then visited a number of stores and played with their model phones and I did some research on the internet to discover what other phones matched my criteria
- 2nd Test: I compared the facilities of all the phones with my original list of criteria
- Exit: I then made my choice and exited the strategy with my purchase

What often happens at the Operate stage is that new criteria are added to our list of requirements. For example, if I discovered some phones with different features than those on my list, I would have to re-cycle back to the 1st test, reset my criteria and start again. This, then, is a model to move from your current state to a desired state.

Take our culture change example. We are aiming to make our current state change to equal to our desired state. The TOTE would look something like this:

- 1st Test: You specify the features of the desired culture and ask yourself if your organisation is there yet? Answer would be 'no we are not'

- Operate: Next you take action and apply different 'operations' that move you closer to your desired state

- 2nd Test: As you journey along you apply another T (test) and ask the question again 'are we there yet?'

- You continue looping around Steps 2 and 3, the Operation and Test, until you reach your desired state

- Exit: Then you exit

If you are not getting the results that you want, it's a useful technique for identifying why you have not yet reached your 'desired state'. Eliciting the step-by-step detail of your strategy will enable you to discover the exact moment the strategy needs to be amended or changed to get you the result that you require.

Strategies for successful culture change

What I'm going to take you through now is an approach to culture change that I've developed over many years of working with clients to deliver the holy grail – a sustainable culture change initiative that delivers long-term change. (The communications and stakeholder management elements of this strategy also apply to any other change project that you might be leading).

Step 1: Align culture with business strategy

Whilst this is a relatively passive step in the strategy it is still important to define the 'desired state'. In Exercise 25 (see Chapter 7), you defined the logical levels of change. These are vital in any culture change programme as you systematically set out the mission, vision and purpose, values and beliefs, capabilities, behaviours and environment that align and reinforce the strategic direction of your business. In terms of level of effort and impact, this step probably takes approximately 10% of the effort of your culture change initiative and has little impact on its own. Yet it sets a firm foundation for change. For example, I'm sure you've been involved in those culture change efforts where a new set of values and behaviours has been pinned on the office wall. This action of itself does not lead to culture change, but it does set a direction of travel that can be reinforced by the following steps.

Step 2: Actively communicate the new logical levels of change

Active communication is an essential component of any culture change programme. Within this step are two sub-steps:

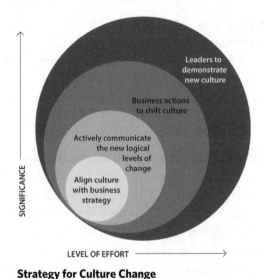

SIGNIFICANCE

Leaders to demonstrate new culture

Business actions to shift culture

Actively communicate the new logical levels of change

Align culture with business strategy

LEVEL OF EFFORT ⟶

Strategy for Culture Change

- Define your stakeholder groups
- Develop your communications strategy and plan

Define your stakeholder groups

In any change process, and in particular a culture change, you have to decide whether you will achieve your changes through compliance or commitment. Both routes require investment. The compliance route usually requires investment in processes to administer, monitor and, if necessary, enforce compliance. Commitment, on the other hand, needs investment in winning hearts and minds, in leaders' time and in communicating with and responding to the workforce. Both routes have their place, and you must pick the right route for the change process to work. The route you choose depends on (a) the kind of change and (b) the level of commitment you need for the change to be successful. In culture change, winning the hearts and minds of stakeholders is vital. Both incur cost, but at different stages. With compliance, heavy costs can occur later on, if old habits return. With commitment, costs occur early on through involving people, communications and stakeholder management.

As a management consultant I was taught an effective way of defining stakeholder groups which you can work through now.

Exercise 30: Defining your stakeholders

Brainstorm all those individuals and groups impacted by the culture change programme.

Then map each person or group onto the grid below. This is done by assessing two dimensions. Firstly, the likely reaction to the change – i.e. are they a potential blocker, still on the fence or a champion of the changes? Secondly, assess their level of power and influence vis-á-vis your project, i.e. is it high, medium or low?

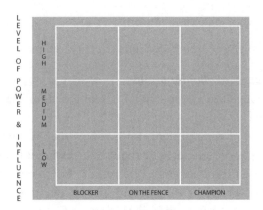

REACTION TO CHANGE

Stakeholder Map

Look at your map. Those on the top right-hand side (champions with high levels of power and influence) are going to be very useful to you in achieving the benefits of the culture change initiative. Those in the top left-hand corner, however, are likely to cause the greatest challenges. Those in the top middle need to be influenced to support you and not be allowed to move into a blocker position. Those at lower levels of power and influence are not to be ignored. Large groups of people with low levels of power who are still blockers can be a very high risk. They can sabotage your initiative. Groups of champions with low levels of power can be a powerful tool to influence other less positive front-line staff.

Make a note below of:

- how you can utilise your champions
- which 'on the fencers' do you absolutely need to get on side, and
- which blockers need to have their power diluted?

A word of warning

Be careful how you use this assessment. I once put a large stakeholder map on the wall in our consulting team's work space at the client site. Unfortunately, someone whom we had assessed as a key 'blocker' came to visit unexpectedly. He was very surprised to discover himself on our chart. That took some explaining! Obviously, it's best to be able to map stakeholders in an open way at a workshop where all key players can express their views.

Develop your communications strategy and plan

Once your stakeholder map is in place, a communications strategy is created to tailor the communications to each specific audience by considering:

- What are the overall objectives and desired outcomes of your communications strategy?

- Who are your audiences?

- What are the key messages you want to tailor to each audience?

- What distribution methods and channels will you use (e.g. intranet using weekly updates)?

- How often will you communicate?

- Who is responsible for the preparation and delivery of each different method?

- How will you monitor the impact of each communication and obtain feedback from each audience?

- What performance measures are you going to set to measure the effectiveness of the communications campaign?

Exercise 31: Developing your communications strategy

Use the template below to assist you to work out your communications strategy.

Communications strategy

	Audience 1	Audience 2	Audience 3	Audience 4	Audience 5	Audience 6
Objectives						
Desired outcomes						
Key messages						
Distribution methods and channels						
Frequency						
Who is responsible for preparation and delivery						
Key impact and feedback measures						

Exercise 32: Developing your communications plan

Use the template below to assist you to work out your communications plan.

Communications plan

Activities:					
Week 1					
Week 2					
Week 3					
Week 4					
Week 5					
Week 6					
Week 7					
Week 8					
etc					

In terms of level of effort and impact, this step probably takes approximately 20% of the effort of your culture change initiative. It begins to have an impact on your business as staff receive targeted communications that build a compelling case for change and highlight benefits (including any dis-benefits) for them. However, these initial two stages will not in themselves deliver a strategy for long-term change because there is still no real incentive for staff to do anything differently and commit to the change process.

Step 3: Take business actions to shift the culture

By the end of Steps 1 and 2, staff understand what needs to change and why. Step 3 is all about how to reinforce those changes at an organisational level. A key example is changing HR policies and procedures to align to the changes. For example:

- Performance management
- Reward and recognition
- Recruitment
- Promotion
- Dealing with those staff members who continually demonstrate resistance

These changes will speed up the culture change process and ensure that changes are embedded within the business. In my experience, too many culture change initiatives miss out this vital step. They define the new world and they communicate it. Yet they continue to reward and promote against the old values and behaviours. This sabotages everything that has been achieved so far.

Exercise 33: How will you align your HR policies and procedures?

Make a note below of the policies and procedures that you need to change in your business to reinforce the culture change. You might need to do some research with your HR team to be able to recommend which policies and procedures will have the greatest leverage for change.

This step accounts for approximately 30% of the impact of the change programme and will begin to make a shift in any organisation. However, even this may not be enough if the leaders of the organisation do not actively sponsor and support the process.

Step 4: Leaders to demonstrate the new culture

Achieving cultural change is a difficult and lengthy process but it can be achieved with adequate leadership resolve. Leadership is by far the strongest lever of cultural change, accounting for approximately 40% of the impact of change.

This final step is all about the leaders in your business exemplifying the values, beliefs, capabilities and behaviours they want their staff to demonstrate. So often leaders adopt a 'do as I say' way of behaving and not 'do as I do'. Some even seem to believe that it's OK for them to carry on as before whilst everyone else in their business changes. Nothing sabotages the success of culture change more than this. For example, the leaders are still receiving large pay rises whilst the staff are on a pay freeze. This will bring nothing but harm to a change project. Leaders can be very blinkered to this step. If you are already a leader you can directly influence this process. If you are not yet a leader consider ways that you can influence key stakeholders.

Exercise 34: Building leadership resolve for change

Make a note below of how you and the other leaders in your business can be an example for the change you want to achieve. For example, if your programme is about breaking down hierarchies this might include a sacrifice or two such as the private dining or premium car-park spot. Or it might be making sure you are up to date with all your appraisals and one-to-ones if it's performance management that needs updating, and so on. The bigger the changes that you make, the bigger the leverage in the rest of the business.

How was that? If you aren't horrified about the things you need to change you probably haven't worked hard enough! Let's face it, you don't achieve 40% impact in terms of the longevity of the culture change without making some pretty big shifts.

Using this approach

I worked alongside the CEO of an engineering organisation gearing up to competition with the private sector. It was an 18 month programme change behaviour around four core new competencies – total customer focus, personal effectiveness, balancing risk and reward and developing commercial and financial expertise. There were four key stages to the work:

- **Aligning culture with business strategy:** We held one-to-one interviews and focus groups to determine which behaviours the staff needed to adopt to deliver the business strategy. As the organisation was gearing up for competition, it was crucial that all managers became more commercially focused and willing to take more risks for potentially greater reward. They also needed to become much more customer focused and more effective in their own relationship building skills.

- **Actively communicate the new logical levels of change:** We held a one day conference for all key stakeholders to feedback the results of our initial study and to finalise the new vision and behaviours with them. There was a range of quick wins that came out of this event plus the design of the change programme to deliver the agreed results.

- **Take business actions to shift the culture:** We held a large event for over 100 change agents to assist in the delivery of change. Their role was to engage with staff at all levels to promote the new behaviours throughout the business. They also got involved in many business actions around aligning performance management systems, HR policies and procedures to the new culture.

● **Leaders to demonstrate new culture:** Leaders were asked to create and manage projects aligned to each of the four new behavioural areas. This meant they had real 'skin in the game'. For example, one group was responsible for new customer service initiatives. This spread the word that the leadership was aligned and serious about the change programme. The CEO was also very visible throughout the process.

The project was very successful and the organisation achieved their goal of retaining their scope of work when the contracts were put out to tender.

Pulling it all together

I pointed out at the start of this chapter that culture change is not for the faint hearted. It requires clarity about what should change, focus, determination, courage and resilience. The approach you choose should be highly out of character with your business. Choose methods that create the 'pattern break' effect, i.e. those that stand out in stark contrast to how it is done now. From the outset, take the initiative and keep going or the old culture will begin to dictate the terms and conditions regarding how the change will be carried out. Remember that embedded beliefs, values and patterns of behaviour wield tremendous voltage. It doesn't make any sense to attempt to change the rules of the game according to the old rules. The NLP approach to strategies and culture change that is discussed here will get you to your outcome if you are prepared to keep focused and keep going.

 In High Velocity Culture Change *Price Pritchett and Ron Pound say:*

'Don't even consider culture change unless you're willing to hit hard, go fast and follow through'.

9
DEVELOPING GLOBAL ORGANISATIONS

//

It's clear that the driving forces towards the emergence of global businesses are greater than the restraining forces. These include a greater global openness and a greater acceptance of ideas and products from other cultures, a greater willingness to engage in multilateral action, and a greater recognition that agreement about some shared values is necessary. At an organisational level, managers everywhere are expected to build and successfully lead virtual teams often spanning several continents. This brings the huge challenges of communication across different time zones, how to join up remote workers, finding a shared approach across the rich mosaic of different values and belief systems, and how to manage the performance and development of workers that you rarely meet face to face. Not surprisingly, the primary reason for business failures in today's global world is inadequate information regarding the business environment and lack of understanding of foreign cultures. (Bonthos, 1994)

In this chapter, you will learn the core competencies required to build and lead virtual teams successfully and how NLP can assist you in this challenge. We'll reflect back over some of the NLP strategies you've learned already and introduce new ones such as Mehrabian's work on the the impact of communication from a verbal and non-verbal perspective. Everything you learned about meta programmes and values in Chapter 5 'Constructing a High Performing Team', is also relevant here.

Here are the competencies that in my experience are critical in leading a world-class virtual team:

- Effective communication
- Performance management and coaching
- Managing across cultural boundaries

There are others, of course, such as state-of-the-art information technology and developing and adapting standard team processes. However, these are outside the scope of this discussion.

What's the extent of your challenge?

Let's begin by assessing the level of complexity in your current situation. You can find out more by completing this from the perspective of the virtual team you manage or your virtual business.

Exercise 35: How complex is your situation?

My business/team...

- Has more than 100 staff   y/n
- Has members from more than one function,
  e.g. production, marketing, sales   y/n
- Is geographically dispersed over three or more
  neighbouring time zones   y/n
- Has members from more than four national cultures   y/n

- Has members whose native language is different
  to other team members   y/n
- Has members who do not have equal access to
  electronic communication   y/n
- Has team members who are more than 4 hours
  travel time apart   y/n
- Is organised in a matrix design structure   y/n

Total number of 'yes' answers:

Complexity Index:

1-2 some complexity

3-5 moderate complexity

6-8 high complexity

The competencies discussed in this chapter are relevant to all levels of global complexity and particularly to those with high complexity.

Effective communication

One of the key discoveries I made as a new manager was that my staff didn't share the same model of the world as me, and they certainly didn't always understand what I was attempting to communicate to them. Typical communication issues in remote teams include allocating meanings to communications which are skewed, leading to misunderstandings, making the wrong assumptions when there is little information to go on, mind-reading what other people are thinking about a situation and getting it wrong, and filling in the communication gaps with the wrong data. And that's before you add in cultural differences! It can become a minefield of problems. NLP gives us useful tools for testing out meanings and getting closer to the reality of the situation.

Reviewing the pre-suppositions of NLP

In Chapter 2, 'A Winning State of Mind', we learned about the pre-suppositions or core principles of NLP. It's worth re-visiting those which are vital to the success of virtual teams:

- **Everyone has a different model of the world.** Keep in mind that every team member will operate from a different model to you and to each other. It's important to invest time in understanding their models of the world and what is important to them. This is best done face to face though telephone calls can work too.

- **The meaning of your communication is the response that you get.** If you ask someone in your virtual team to do something and you don't get back the results you expected, it's a sign that you need to communicate differently. It's not their fault if you have not been clear enough with them! Find out the meta programmes of all your team members (see Chapter 4 'Constructing High-performing Teams') and use what you learn from the exercise in your communications with them. I once got very frustrated with a team member who kept sending me back a draft report that didn't address the issues I expected. I later discovered that I'm off-the-scale global and she is off-the-scale specific. She found me too vague when I gave her work to do. It was my responsibility to translate my instructions into language that she understood.

- **People do the best they can with the resources that they have at the time.** This is good to keep in mind when you get those frustrating moments when team members let you down. Ask them what else they need in order to be able to do what you want. Maybe coaching, training or other assistance such as improved IT or revamped process is required.

- **The person with the most flexibility will achieve the most.** Successful leadership of virtual teams requires flexibility, especially in understanding cross-cultural values. If you don't get your result the first time around, change your strategy. Ask questions, discover what you need to know and then have another go. Keep going until you get your result.

- **All behaviour has a positive intention behind it.** This can be helpful when working in multi-cultural teams. You may sometimes be faced with behaviours and beliefs that are tough to understand. In these instances, remember that your team member had a positive intention in what they did – maybe it was positive in the context of their culture and not yours. For example, you might have some very tight deadlines that the Mediterranean members of your team appear to be ignoring. However, they are busy developing a new opportunity with an old colleague which they've forgotten to tell you about as they haven't seen you face to face for months.

The value of these principles is that they help you as a leader to get the learning from situations and move on quickly. In addition, your staff feel supported because you are listening to them. It's good to share these with your team and get them all to work to these principles. Use the Meta Model (Chapter 7) to ask great questions to find out what's really going on.

The impact of our communication

You learned a little about Mehrabian's work in Chapter 3 'Modelling World-class Performance', and I want to expand on it here in the context of virtual teams. Albert Mehrabian wrote in *Silent Messages* that understanding the difference between words and meaning is a vital capability for effective communications and relationships. His model is particularly useful in illustrating the importance of factors other than words alone when trying to convey meaning (as the speaker) or interpret meaning (as the listener). Style, expression, tonality, facial expression and body language accounted for 93% of the meaning inferred by the people in his studies. In fact, he discovered that words account for 7%, voice tonality 38% and body language 55%. Voice tonality and body language taken together total 93%. So, if I tell you that I'm really excited about something but I'm talking in a slow monotone voice, and if I'm slumped in a chair looking bored as I talk, you are likely to put more far more faith in the tone of my voice and my body language than you are in my words.

This is really important for virtual teams where most of the communication is by email. Remember that up to 93% of the impact can be lost because your team members do not have the added advantage of checking what is being said against body language and tonality, etc.

Let's explore the different channels of communication available to a virtual team:

● **Email.** This is the most popular channel for virtual teams as it gets over the time zone issue. Yet the risks are whether the receiver has actually understood what you meant. Much mis-communication comes from emails. They are full of ambiguities and mind-reads that lead to chaos. So, what to do? It's important to check understanding and interpretation of your instructions, preferably via a telephone call. Ask questions such as 'what did they understand by your email?' 'What specific actions are they going to take as a result?' 'What is the deliverable they will send to you?' and so on. Checking understanding will save lots of errors and frustration in the long run. You cannot assume just because you have sent an email that you will get back what you want. Remember, it's your responsibility to check interpretation.

- **Telephone calls.** Call centre workers estimate that voice tonality accounts for 84% over the phone and words 16%. Again, what is important is to check interpretation while you have the receiver of your communication on the telephone. Using the telephone is also much better for building rapport than an impersonal email. Of course, with the virtual team you have to pick your moment when it is possible to speak across time zones. However, it's well worth the effort.

- **Face-to-face meetings.** These are still by far the best way to communicate as the receiver can align all the elements of your communication and so can you with them. Of course, it's less than easy to meet regularly face to face if you are leading a virtual team. My advice is to always have a face-to-face set-up meeting of a new team or project group to enable members to start to build rapport and relationships. It's worth the investment of time and money to do this. Then schedule in other meetings when you can. After the kick-off meeting use video conferencing whenever possible. A friend of mine was interviewed the other day in London by a team in Sydney, Australia. She said that it felt like they were all in the same room together. Technology has moved on so much that this is a viable option now. If your business doesn't yet have the facility, ask yourself how can you put a business case together for the investment? It will save you days of wasted effort in the end.

Begin to pay attention to all three modes of communication and share this with your staff too. You may need to be creative in terms of time zones to make telephone calls or to hold a virtual video team meeting, yet being more flexible is one of the key competencies for a leader of a global business.

New meta programmes for virtual teams

I want to share with you two more meta programmes that are especially relevant for virtual teams. They are around our listening and speaking styles. These are very relevant for cross-cultural teams, where the local cultures also part a key role in communication (for example, the Americans are very literal speakers and listeners whereas the English tend to be inferential listeners and speakers). Ask yourself the following questions:

- **Listening style:** If someone you knew quite well said to you 'I'm cold' would you:

    a. find the comment interesting, but probably do nothing about it; or

    b. feel compelled to do something about it (e.g. get up and turn the heating on)?

If you answered 'yes' to (a) you are more likely to be a 'literal' listener. This means that you take things literally and would not have taken any action in this instance unless you had been specifically asked to do something. If you answered 'yes' to (b) you are more likely to be an 'inferential' listener. This means that you 'infer' things from what someone else says and take action without being asked. I was helping one of my coaches running the resource table at one of my NLP trainings last year. I said, 'I wonder what's happened to the key to the petty cash tin?' I was merely curious as to where the key could be. The next moment she had disappeared and was searching for the key. She is an inferential listener.

If you have inferential listeners in your virtual team you are likely to have some challenges especially when much communication is not face to face. If you find that your team members are going off and taking inappropriate actions this may be the reason why. Again, it's up to you to qualify exactly what you mean when you give instructions as the risk is that much time and resources may be wasted in misunderstandings. If you have literal listeners then you are going to need to be very direct with them about what you want them to do or they will ignore you.

- **Speaking style**. If you felt that someone around you was not performing as well as they should, would you:

    a. come to the point directly; or

    b. hint, imply and give them clues?

If you answered 'yes' to (a) you are a 'literal' speaker, i.e. you are very direct in your approach. If you answered 'yes' to (b) you are more of an 'inferential' speaker. Both styles have their own challenges. Literal speakers can often offend with their direct style; inferential speakers can cause havoc because no-one really understands what they are getting at.

Let's explore a few scenarios:

- A boss who is an inferential speaker is performance managing a team member who is a literal listener. The boss keeps dropping hints at what needs to change in the other's behaviour and then gets frustrated when the team member doesn't respond. For example, the boss says something like: 'Have you seen the new behaviours for your grade? I thought the ones on customer service were really good, didn't you?' The team member changes nothing about their behaviour towards customers because they don't receive the communication as an instruction. Add the virtual team dimension to this and you have a potentially chaotic scenario which can very quickly get out of hand.

- A team member who is a literal speaker and listener upsets another team member who is an inferential speaker and listener. The receiver thinks the communicator is downright rude. Yet all they said was something like, 'Can I give you some feedback? If you spend less time on the internet and more time out visiting clients you'd get better results'. Situations like this can rapidly break down into a grievance scenario that you as the manager have then to unravel.

Find out the styles of your team members either by observation or by asking them. Notice your own style and practice becoming more flexible across the styles – especially inferential to literal. There are times when a literal style is very important to ensure that boundaries are clear and instructions are understood.

Performance management and coaching

The success of global businesses and virtual teams is often dependent upon establishing clear principles and boundaries that enable a self-directed working style and the team to continue working effectively in the absence of an 'on the spot' manager. This is how NLP can help to set your principles and boundaries within which the team or business will operate:

- Develop the logical levels of change for your team with input from team members and other key stakeholders (see Chapter 7). This should be the core agenda of your face-to-face kick-off meeting. This sets an agreed mission, vision, purpose, beliefs, values, capabilities, behaviours and environment for the team. This then, becomes the Team Charter against which future interactions can be assessed.

- Clearly define the goals and priorities of the team and agree them with team members (see Chapter 4).

- It is important to agree the accountability of the team members in relation to each other. Using the principles of cause and effect (see Chapter 2) and getting each team member to take 100% responsibility for the results of the team will ensure that important decisions get taken and are followed through.

- At the kick-off meeting, discuss the different cultures within the team and how national culture will play a role in team interaction. Be open and candid about stereotypes and ask team members to predict what may happen. Involve team members in agreeing strategies for dealing with intercultural behaviours. For example, if you have British team members, discuss the fact that they tend to be inferential speakers and listeners and the possible implications of this.

- Identify results-orientated performance measures and rewards for the team as a whole as well as for each individual to ensure that all team members, no matter where they are based, are focused on the success of the whole team and not just their individual success.

- Develop methods to review progress and results, e.g. weekly conference calls or video meetings. It is important that all team members are kept engaged and motivated so frequent meetings, however achieved, will pay dividends.

- Establish a coaching culture and train team members as coaches using the coaching model shared in Chapter 6. This will guarantee that all staff continue to be developed whether or not you are physically there. Ensure that all team members receive regular one-to-one coaching sessions and that you review regularly to ensure these are happening.

- Give timely feedback about performance to each local team and to individual team members. Avoid the danger of giving feedback when you next see them face to face. Do it on the spot using the telephone or video meeting. Use one of the feedback models we discussed in Chapter 6. Avoid email for all the reasons discussed earlier.

● Agree ways of modelling best practices between teams (see Chapter 3). So if one team gets excellent results, find out what they did differently and share with all other teams.

Always remember that results are accomplished through people. Networking, keeping people informed, soliciting input from team members, stakeholders and customers will always be an important part of your role. Investing time and energy into the set-up of virtual teams and businesses will reap rewards in the longer term. Clear policies and practices to manage the team as well as motivational goals and regular feedback will enable you to direct behaviour and performance from a distance. You will build the trust of your team through your own reliability and consistency of approach.

Managing across cultural boundaries

A global mindset involves two key issues – an understanding of cross-cultural competencies as well as global, political, social and economic factors. We are going to focus here on developing cross-cultural awareness because it is on the front line, where culture leads business practices, that cultural awareness can be the difference between the success or failure of global teams. There are many different studies of the differences between national cultures – Hofestede and Trompenaars have written some of the most famous. For the purposes of this book, here's just a flavour of some of the common cultural traits that I have observed and modelled from many years of working with global businesses. They are, of course, generalisations so do not expect to discover these traits in everyone. However, they are a useful guideline to open discussions with your virtual team.

Cultural differences in business

Country	Traits	Strategies for success
England	Individualism, deference and inequality, self-control and reserve, conservatism, honesty and trust, liberty and class-consciousness, emotions controlled, cool, work very important, inferential communicators, pragmatic	Ask questions for clarity, check understanding, discover their 'informal' networks. Give them structure, rules and deadlines though you may find that they may break them. Use humour to break through 'coolness'
US	Very focused on achievement, keeping distance/space, highly mobile, direct communication, spirited individualism, shared philosophy and beliefs	Match their direct communication style. Focus on results. Use a coaching style and show patience. Demonstrate concern for the morale of the team. Give them a less detailed structure with more room for variation.
France	Up front and differentiated, think in a complicated way, innately suspicious, never forget business process, have strong reservations, do not like mechanical approaches, flexible and less attached to specific business, can be direct and rude, argumentative	Difficult to convince, need lots of evidence. Qualifications and titles are important to them. Direct approach is best. Build relationships outside of work – mealtimes are important.

(Continued)

Country	Traits	Strategies for success
Germany	Collective in nature, pragmatic in approach, advanced in technology and technological application, strong authority, self-sufficiency, logical and rational approaches	Give them structure, rational approaches, plans. Be firm with them and focus on the task, not the people. Stress goals and demonstrate urgency. Be on time for meetings.
China	Collectivism, self-sufficient, individually accomplished, more theoretical, non-empirical, globally conscious, some still believe in Confucian value, love to be incentivised, relatively open	Allow them to save face. Do not challenge in a group, be detailed and precise, process as important as result, need to encourage individuals to stand out, take time to build work relationships.
India	Advanced in Information Technology. High emotional power, obedient to seniors, dependent, fatalist, reserved, community oriented, collective responsibility, more friendly, less tenacious, clan superiority, class consciousness, law abiding, sensitive	Be clear about what you need and check understanding. Give credit and regularly check progress. Often very bright individuals who need lots of evidence to be convinced.

(Continued)

Country	Traits	Strategies for success
Latin countries	Warm, friendly, more laid back and spontaneous, work to live, use networking to get things done, like to socialise, time is not important as the process, chaotic yet bureaucratic, lively and direct	Need to keep them on track and explain why. Don't challenge the boss publically. Match their lively and direct style as everything will be forgotten later. Be deferential to the hierarchy. Be warm and friendly with them. Important to socialise and make friends.

A new entente cordiale

I was running a cultural awareness session as part of a 5-day Advanced Management Programme for a global electronics business. The business had been formed by the merger between a French and an Italian company – an interesting mix. The group took the opportunity to ask me questions about the English culture. I was taken aback when a senior French manager asked me the following question: 'Why are the English such liars?' I asked him to tell me more about where his belief came from. He explained that the English staff in his team never told him what they were really thinking and often said one thing to be polite and then would go off and do something completely different! He was frustrated and angry with their behaviour and it threatened the success of his team. I thought it was a very interesting example of the differences between the English and the French. I explained that the English are inferential listeners and speakers and would find it very hard to be direct with him. They would believe that was very rude behaviour. So they would be likely to agree or be very vague to end the communication. Then they would find a pragmatic way behind the scenes of dealing with the situation. I asked him how he could change his behaviour towards them (ref: NLP pre-supposition: 'the meaning of the communication is the response you get'). After much debate, he said he would coach the English to be more open and direct with him and to tell him what was really going on for them. I heard later that the relationships were much improved.

Exercise 36: Planning for global performance

Plan the agenda for your next virtual team meeting or a new kick-off meeting. Make sure that all the issues of your team charter are addressed. Pay particular attention to building awareness of and resolving cross-cultural issues, improving team performance and communication skills. Make a note of the agenda items below:

Pulling it all together

The stakes are high in global virtual teams which in itself can create tension from risk of failure. The language and communication abilities, the challenge of managing performance from a distance and the culture-specific mindsets are all obstacles in the path of a leader within a developing global business. However, enabling strategies such as setting clear goals and outcomes, specifying expectations about working methods and creating an openess about cultural differences in the early days will pay dividends. Teams which benefit from an understanding of the potential issues and that have a shared vision, values and behaviours are much more likely to find creative ways of working together. Leaders need to understand that from start to finish everything has a cultural twist to it. As far as possible, this twist should be addressed specifically although it should also be on your mind that any issue can be more loaded with culture than assumed and needs to be handled in a sensitive manner. This constant readiness to be flexible will help turn you into a successful leader of any global business.

 Never assume that staff speaking the same language from different countries share the same culture!

PART FOUR

Transforming Customer Service with NLP

10

INFLUENCING WITH INTEGRITY

'Customer service is those activities provided by a company's employees that enhance the ability of a customer to realise the full potential value of a product or service before and after the sale is made, thereby leading to satisfaction and repurchase.'

Rosanne D'Ausilio, TMCnet Call Centre Training
Columnist for CRM and *Marketing Magazine*

The first three parts of this book have focused the spotlight internally on what you need to do to develop your own leadership skills, how to build a world-class team and how to implement successful change inside your business. This last part of the book refocuses the spotlight externally. It's all about how to build world-class customer service and long-term relationships. It is very costly in both time and money to bring in new business. Clearly, keeping your current customers and building lasting relationships where your customers continue to choose you as their supplier is by far the most cost effective and rewarding solution. New customers, when they do appear, then come via word of mouth and reputation rather than costly advertising and competition. In the public sector, where all large contracts have to go to competition, our strategy at The Change Corporation has been to build relationships to ensure that we are invited to tender for admission onto preferred supplier lists. This reduces the complexity of the competition and improves our chances of success considerably.

The overall aim is to have clients 'pull' your services from you as opposed to you going out and 'pushing' them. This is the missing piece that, along with the other three parts, builds a complete toolkit to transform your business. In this chapter, you will explore how to influence with integrity using other major elements of NLP such sensory acuity and rapport, how to identify different communication styles and translate your communications to match theirs, and interpret what people are thinking via their eye patterns.

NLP – manipulation or influence?

One question I get asked more than any other is whether or not NLP is manipulative. I often challenge those who pose the question by asking if they know of any sales people who have been taught 'manipulative' techniques. Of course they have, so NLP is not the only toolkit that has the potential to manipulate – there are many sales people out there with huge sales targets who are taught to sell at all costs, whether the customer needs the goods or not. I would, therefore, agree that the potential is there in NLP. Indeed, you have already learned some very powerful techniques and you will learn some more in this chapter. What makes the difference is how you use the tools you have been taught. That's why this chapter is entitled 'Influencing with Integrity'. The difference between manipulation and influence is actually simple. Genie Z Laborde describes it as follows:

> 'Once you know how to clarify your own desires (or outcomes) you can use the same techniques to clarify the outcomes of any other party involved in the communication. Achieving that party's outcome while you achieve your own is what I call influencing with integrity'.

In contrast, achieving your outcome at the expense of another constitutes manipulation. For example, selling to achieve your target to customers who do not need or want your service is manipulation. In contrast, making your sales target by selling to customers who want your service and would gain value from it, is influencing with integrity. That's the real difference. We also know from the principles of NLP, that if we operate from a positive intention for our customer then we are going to get a 'win win' result.

How to use NLP to influence with integrity

Essentially there are three core skills which add up to improving your own emotional intelligence and ability to communicate more effectively with your customers:

- The first skill is *sensory acuity*. You need to develop an acute sense of awareness of what is going on around you moment to moment, spot those changes in your customer's physiology and work out what they mean for your interaction with them. You will learn in this chapter how to see, hear and feel more than most people do.

- The second skill is *rapport building*. You need to develop a way of building a strong connection with your customers, fast. In fact, in NLP we often say that any sign of resistance in your customer is a sign to you of a lack of rapport. You will learn in this chapter how to build rapport with the majority of the people that you meet.

- The third skill is *flexibility*. We've already learned about how to spot and respond to different behavioural styles in Chapter 4. In this chapter we'll build on that by learning about eye patterns and communication styles. You will develop your flexibility by learning how to spot different eye patterns and communication styles and then responding differently in the moment. This will build your flexibility in influencing others and help to build amazing rapport with the other person in the moment.

Let's begin with sensory acuity.

Improving your sensory awareness

> ## Missing the vital signs
>
> I was training a group of senior sales people for a global IT products and services business. One exercise involved them working in pairs and learning to coach each other. At the last minute I asked the Finance Director, who had arrived to open the event, to stand in and coach as we had odd numbers. I observed him giving coaching to a young female sales person. I noticed that she was beginning to react to his questioning. Her breathing quickened, her face flushed and her eyes filled with tears. I waited for the FD to react and change tact or check that she was OK. Nothing happened and I realised that he was completely oblivious to what was going on with her. I called a 'time-out' and asked him what he was noticing in his coachee. He had noticed nothing until I pointed out the changes in her physiology.

Sadly, I was to learn that seniority is no guarantee of good sensory acuity. We all have varying levels of sensory acuity. What I mean by this is how we intuitively pick up non-verbal signals in others. You have probably had an experience where you went to ask the boss for a favour and then decided it was not the right time because of some signals you picked up from them. Increasing your sensory acuity will improve how you communicate with everyone and especially with your customers as you begin to predict how others are about to react.

What's most important is to notice minute changes in others from moment to moment. Our internal thoughts are expressed through our external behaviour. Internal thoughts and emotions literally 'leak' out of our physiology. Remember, 55% of the impact of our communication is non-verbal. You cannot not communicate. However, you also need to learn how to calibrate these changes. Calibration is the recognition of a change in the physiology of someone you are dealing with moment to moment from their non-verbal signals. For example, if someone you are chatting to suddenly turns bright red in the face you might interpret that as anger. However, that is your mind-read based on your own experiences and perceptions. You will need to check out your interpretation with them. For example, I noticed one of my students tensing their forehead in the training room. It looked like they might be bored. However, that was my mind-read. In the break I asked him if everything was going OK. He explained that he was having to concentrate really hard and was enjoying the training. So my mind-read of boredom was wrong – it was actually concentration. That's why a sensory description and then calibration is so important. The alternative is your mind-read and imagination.

Why would you want to improve your sensory acuity? If you take your customers, you can begin to do two things. With someone you've never met before you can pick up changes in their physiology and then you need to explore what might be going on for them. For example, if you tell a customer your view about something and you see their face flush it tells you that something has changed for them. You might then ask them a question such as 'How do you feel about that?' Secondly, if you know a client well you might already be able to start to calibrate from changes in their physiology what is really going on for them. You can start to predict how they might be about to react. In my earlier example, once I'd calibrated with my student that a frown meant concentration I would then know that next time I saw him frown he was concentrating really hard.

Recognising the non-verbals

Here are some reactions to watch out for:

- Skin colour changes from light to dark or vice versa

- The tone of the skin might go from not shiny to shiny or vice versa

- The breathing might change both in terms of rate and location (people breathe high in the chest, low in the chest, at the waist and deep into the abdomen)

- The eyes might go from focused to unfocused or vice versa, or the pupil dilation may change

- The lower lip appearance might go from lines to no lines or vice versa

- Or anything else you can see!

It also helps to use your peripheral vision as you will notice more. Peripheral vision is what you use when you are driving. It allows you to take in a much broader perspective. Foveal vision, in contrast, is more like tunnel vision – it's very focused and less useful for developing your sensory acuity skills as too much information is outside of your awareness.

///

Exercise 37: Improve your sensory acuity

Lie detector

Find someone willing to work with you on this.

- Person A is the speaker, Person B is the guesser
- A makes 5 true statements, then 5 false statements. They tell B which they are saying

- B must begin to calibrate their physiology when they are telling the truth and any differences when they lie
- A then makes random statements and B uses their new-found 'extra' sensory acuity to answer after each statement whether it was true or false.
- Person B needs to get three correct 'guesses'in a row

Who am I thinking about?

Work with the same partner:

- A is the thinker, B the guesser
- B asks A to think of someone he/she likes very much. Then B asks A to think of someone he/she really dislikes. It's important to make each example intense, i.e. someone you really like and someone you really dislike
- Person A tells person B which they are thinking of, i.e. they say, 'I'm thinking of the person I like'. Then they just think of that person for several seconds. They keep going until person B believes they have calibrated the difference in person A's physiology between the two
- A then thinks of either person at random without saying anything, and B must guess which person A is thinking of
- Person B needs to score three correct 'guesses' in a row

How was that? Were you surprised at how quickly you can begin to sharpen your sensory acuity skills? Excellent sensory acuity is the basis of all world-class communication and the foundation for good rapport. You need good sensory acuity to know if you are either in or out of rapport with someone. Signs will tell you if you are on track or not. Don't be like our Financial Director in the case study. Take time each day to practise your sensory acuity skills. Notice those minute moment-to-moment physiological shifts and begin to calibrate what they mean. Your skills will improve quickly. As for the Financial

Director – well, he left soon after and I often wondered if the feedback he got that day hastened his departure.

What is rapport?

'Rapport is a somewhat exotic English word derived from the French verb *rapporter*, meaning to bring back or refer. The English meaning – a relation of harmony, conformity, accord, or affinity – indicates the importance of rapport to communication. It is the most important process in any interaction…without rapport you will not get what you want – not money, promotions, not friends.' Genie Z Laborde

In NLP we say that any resistance in a customer, or any other person with whom we are communicating, is a sign of a lack of rapport. It's our signal that we need to be flexible and do something different with our communication.

Why should we want to be in rapport in the first place? The key advantages of rapport are that the other person (or group) will listen to us more readily, feel comfortable in the communication and, most importantly, be more likely to accept our suggestions to them. How do you know that you have rapport? Well, four things are likely to happen: you will feel it by a certain level of comfort, you may notice a colour shift in yourself or the other person, they might say something like 'I feel like I've known you for ages', or you might notice that if you shift your physiology they will follow you. This is called 'leading in NLP'. When people are in rapport you will also notice that their bodies are in a similar position, i.e. they are matching each other's physiology. That's because, unconsciously, when we feel we are 'like' someone we are more inclined to 'like' them. For example, if you go into a pub on a Saturday night you can see the people who are unconsciously in rapport because their bodies will be matching. You do not have to hear what they are saying to know this. Equally, if they are out of rapport their bodies will be mismatching each other. That's why, when you see a couple arguing, they tend to break eye contact. So we build rapport unconsciously as a natural behaviour. The aim here is to bring it into your awareness and to turn it into more of a conscious behaviour – i.e. you take control of the behaviour and use it with volition.

Rapport building with customers

Andrew Neville talks about his rapport-building skills after the completion of his Practitioner certification:

'Before I looked seriously at NLP, my meetings would be generally about making sure that I was understood and had got across what I wanted to my customer, with their response or consideration of the response a secondary issue. By listening to customers, understanding their points of view, matching their physiology and using their language, seeking to understand rather than to be understood, the meeting changed completely. A meeting that would have normally lasted an hour lasted over two hours. I learned more meaningful information about their business, to the extent that I now understand far better than before how their business works, and I gave them the time to really explain – this led to my understanding that our solutions to what I thought were their problems were wrong. I therefore could match our solution far better to their needs and be far more likely to make the sale. If I had not established rapport building then I would have been unlikely to get the same level of commitment from the customer that was actually achieved. After that meeting, I also got more opportunities to supply more products – the customer wanted to talk to me more!'

How do you build rapport?

In Chapter 9, you learned that the impact of communication is made up of three elements: words, tonality and physiology. You are going to practise building rapport using all three channels. You will begin with physiology because it has the biggest impact (55%). We have seen that when people are alike, they match each other. Building effective and lasting rapport involves using your sensory acuity to observe what they are doing with their physiology and you choose a couple of elements to effectively 'copy'.

Physiology

These are the elements you watch out for:

- Posture:
  - angle of spine when sitting
  - head/shoulder relationship
  - upper body position.
  - lower body position
- Gestures
- Facial expression and blinking
- Breathing:
  - rate
  - location

If your customer has their left leg over their right leg you do the same – that is matching. If you put your right leg over your left leg, that is mirroring as it's a mirror image of the other person. Although it may appear strange and you may worry that the other party will catch you out, don't worry. Because we build rapport unconsciously all the time, no one will ever spot it. Be subtle though. It's over the top to match every part of their physiology. Just pick a few things in the beginning and notice what happens. Facial expressions mean that if you have a customer who uses lots of facial expressions you do the same when you speak. You don't have to match their expressions exactly – do what feels comfortable. It's the same for gestures. If you are communicating with someone who uses a lot of gestures, make sure you add some to your communication when you speak. You will know when you have rapport, because when you change your position they will follow you. You are then leading them. When you have rapport you will begin to notice how easy it is to get agreement with them.

Exercise 38: Matching body postures

Start to match physiology in many different circumstances – with customers, at work, at home – and notice what happens. If you get into a challenging situation, start to match and mirror and notice how the disagreement begins to dry up. If you want to end a meeting quickly, start to mismatch physiology and you'll soon get your outcome! Experiment and notice what happens. Write your results below:

Voice tonality

Tonality accounts for 38% of the impact of communication. Genie Z Laborde says that 'matching the other person's voice tone or tempo is the best way to establish rapport in the business world.'

Tones are high or low, loud or soft, and tempo is fast or slow, sometimes with pauses. This is also the main way to build rapport over the telephone. You do not have to match the voice exactly, just close enough for the other person to feel a sense of familiarity. Don't match accents – that is a recipe for disaster. Use your sensory acuity to begin to notice the differences in tonality. In a situation where the other person is shouting, you should raise your tone, i.e. move closer to them. In the past, customer services staff have been taught to be quiet and encourage the person to quieten down when they are angry. However, in NLP, it is felt that this has the impact of mismatching and is more likely to fuel the situation.

Exercise 39: Matching voice tonality

Start to match voice tempo first. Notice different rates of speech. Later move on to matching tones. If you get into a challenging situation, start to match tempo and tone and notice how quickly the disagreement begins to dry up. Experiment often with this to build your flexibility. Notice what happens. Write your results below:

Words

Finally, let's discover how to match words. There are a number of things to listen out for. We're going to learn how to identify different communication styles and match the style our customer is using. In addition, listen out for key words that the person uses over and over again. Start to use them in your language. Listen out for common experiences, interests and values that you share and bring them into the conversation. Don't pretend though – there is too high a risk that you'll come unstuck! Also, notice the content chunks that they use, i.e. do they use short or long sentences? Modify your content chunks to match theirs.

Representational systems

The second major NLP pattern discovered by Bandler and Grinder is that of 'representational systems'. In business I translate this as communication styles as it's easier for people to understand. It all started when Bandler and Grinder noticed three different types of patterning in language. They noticed that people spoke using visual, auditory or kinaesthetic words (or predicates as they are called in NLP). They already knew, of course, that people structure their experience of the world through the five senses: seeing, hearing, feeling, tasting and smelling. They began to realise that there was a link to a matching set of 'internal senses' which they later called Representational Systems. In other words, they discovered that each of our sensory inputs had physical places in our brains to which the experience is sent, processed and recorded. Lewis and Pucelik argued that:

> 'what we actually perceive are representations or models of what each of our sensory organs transmits to us. These individual models of assimilation are called representational systems.'

Another way of describing these would be as preferences in our thinking patterns. For example, if I say the word 'sea', what comes to your mind? Do you see a picture of the sea, or hear the sound of the waves or remember the feeling of hot sand under your toes? Although we all use all of these representational systems, you will find that you do have a preference towards one of these styles. For example:

- If you saw an image of the sea first the chances are that you have a **Visual** preference. You process information in pictures. Things have to 'look' right to you for you to take action.

- If you heard the sound of the sea first the chances are that you have an **Auditory** preference. You process information through sounds. Things have to 'sound' right for you to take action.

- If you felt the hot sand beneath your feet first the chances are that you have a **Kinaesthetic** preference. You process through your feelings. Things have to 'feel' right to you for you to take action.

- If you were reminded of some interesting facts and statistics about the sea the chances are that you have an **Audio Digital** preference. Though not one of the styles identified by Bandler and Grinder, the 'digital' style was added by Lewis and Pucelik. This style processes through logic and what makes sense. ADs can be disassociated from their feelings and they have to understand something and for it to make 'sense' to them before they take action.

What's really fascinating is that each of these representational systems has a set of characteristics that is common to that system. This is very exciting as it means you can start to spot someone's style easily, even if you are on the phone, and you can build great rapport by matching the language and physiology that they use. As you go through the following characteristics and then the language that each system uses, ask yourself 'which is most like you?' and use it to check against the results of the 'sea' experiment above. Also notice which system you feel least comfortable with, because to become a masterful rapport builder, you will need to practise that one the most.

And, please remember that this is a model based on generalisations of behaviour. We are all different so be wary of the potential to become limited by generalisations.

Characteristics of the different representational systems

Visual people:

- Process information faster because they can move between pictures in their heads quickly

- Are thinner than the other styles

- Stand or sit upright with erect spine because they like to see what is going on

- Have higher pitched, loud, fast, clear speech

- Breathe at top of lungs because they speak faster than the other styles

- Like to keep a physical distance between themselves and others to be able to see what's going on

- Are neat, tidy and well groomed – often prefer 'designer' clothes that stand out

- Are not good at memorizing verbal instructions

- Believe that what people/places/things 'look like' is important. Can be disconnected from bodily experiences because the visual portions of their environment command their attention, e.g. physical demands such as hunger can go unnoticed

Kinaesthetic people:

- Breathe from the bottom of their lungs as it takes longer to process information through feelings
- Can be larger physically than Visuals
- Have lower pitched, slower, quieter voices
- Move slowly and deliberately
- Respond to touch and physical reward
- Stand closer than a Visual person as they like the connection
- Memorise by doing and walking through the steps
- More connected to their bodily needs and comforts
- Like to wear comfortable clothes and be in a comfortable environment

Auditory people:

- Tend to be slim
- Are often seen with arms folded and head tilted to one side to listen
- Breathe from the middle of their chest.
- Talk to themselves.
- Are easily distracted by noise
- Can repeat back words exactly
- Like talking on the phone and listening to music
- Memorize things by steps, procedures and sequences
- Are sensitive to tone of voice

Audio digital people:

- Tend to be disassociated from their feelings
- Learn things by making sense of things
- May experience tension in neck and shoulders (as they are in their heads all the time)
- Can take on characteristics of other systems

Remember we all have the ability to behave like any one of these categories at different times so always trust your experience.

Learning to speak a new language

You can also spot what preferences people have from the words or predicates that they use. Appendix 2 lists examples of the types of words each style will primarily use. These words reflect whether they are thinking using their Visual, Auditory, Kinaesthetic or Audio Digital systems, and this gives you an insight into how their brain is sorting information at the time. You can't tell *what* a person is thinking but you can have a good idea *how* they are thinking! For example, Visual people will use words like 'see, clear, illuminate, etc.' and say phrases like 'I can see that'. They are literally telling you that they are making a picture in their minds. A Kinaesthetic person will say words like 'feel, touch, grasp' and use phrases such as 'that feels good to me'. An Auditory person will use words like 'hear, listen, sounds' and phrases like 'that sounds good to me'. An Audio Digital person will use words like 'sense, think, experience' and say phrases like 'that makes sense to me'.

By listening to the words someone uses you can begin to identify their preferred style. This, added to spotting the characteristics we discussed earlier, will make it very easy to identify the style of the person you are communicating with. It is that simple – listen for the representational words which indicate in which style the person is thinking, and adjust your communication style to match. Much miscommunication comes from people mismatching the style of the other person. That breaks rapport. Using the same language as your customer will build rapport with them very quickly. For example, if you keep using auditory words to a Visual person, they will unconsciously have to translate internally to their own system. This takes time, can be difficult for some people, and does not build rapport. You will find that you get along naturally more easily with those people who have the same preference as you. You may have been unknowingly breaking rapport with some of your key your customers up until now.

Exercise 40: Speaking a new language

Start off by picking a significant person in your life and listen to the types of words they use. You will notice they probably use all types of the visual, auditory and kinaesthetic words…but one type will usually predominate. Then practise translating your language to match their system. You may find that translating into a language that is your least preferred style is the biggest stretch for you. That means it's the one you most need to practise.

If they say, 'I don't see your point,' don't say 'Let me repeat it,'; instead say, 'Let me show you what I mean.'

If they say, 'What you're suggesting doesn't feel right to me,' don't say, 'Take a different view,'; instead say, 'Let's touch upon the points another way.'

If they say, 'I've tuned you out,' don't say, 'You're insensitive,'; instead say, 'Let's talk it over.'

Then practise with your customers, and listen to conversations on radio or television to develop your skills. Eventually you will find yourself doing it automatically.

Write your key learning points below:

Light bulb moments

A salesperson in China had an opportunity to sell a very sophisticated piece of machinery worth over 550,000 euros. She only had five minutes to build rapport and impress her client. Her preferred communication style and that of many of her colleagues is audio digital. She began to explain the machine in lots of technical detail. She noticed that her customer seemed distracted. She wondered why. Then she noticed his stylish suit, slim build and interest in what was going on around him. She switched into visual language, explaining more about what the machine looked like and showing him different aspects. He immediately became more interested and she made the deal.

Practice makes perfect

You have now learned how to build rapport using your physiology, tonality and your words. However, the only way to become skilled at this is to practise. By practising consciously you'll soon find that you begin to do things unconsciously. You may be surprised to notice how much you've learned and are already using. And, of course, if you think these skills are just for use with your customers you'd be missing an opportunity to improve all the key relationships in your life.

NLP eye patterns

In the weeks following the discovery of representational systems, Bandler and Grinder recognised something quite

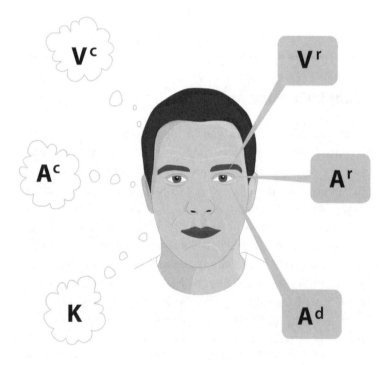

V^c Visual Constructed	V^r Visual Remembered
A^c Auditory Constructed	A^r Auditory Remembered
K Kinaesthetic (Feelings)	A^d Auditory Digital (Self-talk)

NLP Eye Patterns

extraordinary. There are few patterns of NLP that can be claimed to be totally original (as opposed to modelling of world-class behaviour), but the discovery of eye movements is one such pattern. As they had both been totally focused on listening to the predicates used by people, they began to notice that they were, as Grinder described it, 'astonished by the regularity and obviousness of the associated eye patterns'.

They coded their independent observations into what now has become known as the NLP 'funny face'.

N.B this is as you look at the person.

These are the eye patterns of a 'normally' organised person. They are independent of language and culture. Occasionally, people are reverse organised, i.e. their patterns are a mirror image of those shown above. To explain the model, you:

- Look up and to your left when you are remembering an image of something from the past, e.g. your favourite holiday as a child

- Look up and to your right when you are imagining or constructing an image of something, e.g. imagining what you would look like in that new suit/dress

- Look across and to your left when you are remembering a sound from the past, e.g. your favourite sound track

- Look across and to your right when you are constructing a sound, e.g. hearing yourself singing with a strange voice

- Look down and to your left when you are talking to yourself or working out a logical calculation or generating a set of logical criteria

- Look down and to your right when you are into your feelings, e.g. you are feeling happy about something

Exercise 41: Seeing magic

Here is a set of questions that will help you to spot the eye patterns of another person. You'll need a volunteer for this exercise. Ask each question and watch where the eyes of your partner go. You will need to be fast so make sure you memorise the question and then ask it as you are looking at your partner – otherwise you'll miss the action!

Eye pattern elicitation questions

Used with permission Copyright © The Tad James Co, Tad and Adriana James

Visual Remembered [looking up to your left]:

a. What was the colour of the room you grew up in?
b. What was the colour of your front door when you were a kid?

Visual Construct (looking up to your right):

a. What would your room look like if it were painted green with purple spots?

b. What would your car look like with a Rolls Royce radiator grill and turbo go faster stripe?

Auditory Remembered (looking across to your left):

a. What was the last thing I said to you?

b. Can you hear your favourite piece of music all of the time?

Auditory Construct (looking across to your right):

a. What would I sound like with Darth Vader's voice?
b. What would your favourite piece of music sound like played backwards?

Auditory Digital (looking down to your left):

a. What was the first thing you said to yourself this morning?
b. Can you recite your national anthem to yourself?

Kinaesthetic (looking down to your right):

a. What does it feel like to stand barefoot on a wet carpet?
b. What does it feel like to put on a shirt or blouse?

Sometimes you may find things happening that you didn't expect when you ask the questions. Here are some key distinctions to bear in mind:

- If someone has a 'look to listen rule' ask them to turn it off for the exercise and allow their eyes to move around freely

- Some people move their eyes to their 'lead' representational system first. For example, if they have a visual lead system they are likely to move their eyes to visual remembered first to get a picture before they move their eyes elsewhere. It's often the case, but not always, that our preferred representational system is the same as our lead system.

- Some people hear the question again in their mind first and their eyes go to auditory remembered before they move their eyes elsewhere

- Some people repeat the question to themselves first and their eyes go to auditory digital before they move their eyes elsewhere

- If they have had a trauma in the past they may have learnt not to go into their kinesthetic as it doesn't feel good

- Finally, you may spot a synesthesia where two or more representation systems overlap each other. For example, if someone has a visual remembered/kinesthetic synesthesia they will get a feeling whilst seeing a picture so you won't see the kinesthetic eye pattern you'll only see the visual remembered eye pattern whilst hearing them use some kinaesthetic words

These distinctions make it easy for you to get a good result every time you access eye patterns.

Pulling it all together

Using eye patterns, you can literally 'see' what your customers are doing inside their heads from moment to moment. Just imagine how powerful it would be if you saw your customer in their feelings, to match your language at that moment. You could say 'How do you feel about that...'. As if by magic you would build exquisite rapport with them there and then. If you add this to your techniques for sensory acuity and rapport building you have a powerful toolkit to influence your customers in the moment. They will feel amazed at how you can almost read their minds. They will feel comfortable because you appear to be like them and they will be much more likely to accept your suggestions and recommendations because you have rapport. Remember, too, that you use these tools with integrity, to assist your customers make decisions about products and services that they have already told you will be useful to them. That way it's a 'win–win' scenario for both of you.

These tools also enable us to be far more flexible in the moment. Any resistance from our customer is a sign of a lack of rapport and it's your signal to experiment with something different, such as matching physiology, tonality, language or noticing eye patterns. It's an incredible toolkit so use it wisely!

Take every opportunity to practise these tools. You can use the TV or films to begin to notice so much more. Politicians are good to observe. See what you can calibrate about what they are really saying!

11

POWERFUL PRESENTATIONS

///

Have you ever considered that we are all sales people? I say that because we are all selling ideas all of the time. We may be attempting to convince our kids or our partner about where to go on holiday this year or persuading our team at work about a change to existing procedures or pitching to a potential new customer about a major new business deal. Considering that we are always 'pitching' ideas, this chapter is all about how to develop your presentation skills so that you always have the best opportunity to clinch the deal.

Practice in presenting will give you a competitive edge with your customers. The objective in this chapter is for you blow away the opposition in any presentation opportunity and to enjoy the experience at the same time. You may be thinking that this is a little far-fetched. Maybe it feels like that now but by the end of this chapter I guarantee you'll know how to feel relaxed in any presentation situation, be able to structure the perfect presentation in minutes and use your gestures with volition. When people see master presenters they think they are a natural yet this is not the case. Sure, some people are more natural presenters than others, yet anyone can model and learn from people who are naturals. You are going to learn the strategies used by master presenters. Much of what you've already learned is also relevant here so I'm not going to go over it again. Only to say, review the mindset for success, especially the importance of focusing on what you want (Chapter 2), use of language (Chapter 7) and sensory acuity, rapport and the representational systems (Chapter 10). By the way, if you are presenting one-on-one it's important to match the preferred representational system of your partner. If you are presenting to a group, mix up your language so you engage with everyone in the room.

Fear of public speaking

Having to speak in public is reported to be the number one fear of American adults, with many people experiencing tremendous suffering because of it. This fear often takes a huge toll on people's effectiveness both in the workplace and in other settings, as it stops them from fully expressing their thoughts and ideas in front of others. (The number two fear in the US is death, so you might assume that Americans are more afraid of public speaking than dying.) In the UK, the number one fear is reported to be spiders, followed by public speaking at number two. So, in the UK, if you are presenting to a room full of spiders you are really in trouble! Yet to be afraid of public speaking is irrational. Most of it is built up in our heads by focusing on the presentation going badly before we even get there. Or when we are there, we fixate on the one person who doesn't seem to be enjoying our presentation rather than noticing the rest who are.

We have a situation, then, where all of us would benefit from improving our presentation skills because we are making pitches all the time, yet many of us are terrified of standing up and speaking in front of a group. We will start by learning how to relax in front of our audience.

The presenter state

The aim of the 'presenter state' is to be totally present in the moment and to feel calm and balanced on the inside, ready for anything. I was taught the 'presenter state' when I trained as an NLP trainer and I have used it ever since to prepare for every training and presentation that I have done. A few months ago, I was facilitating a day-long conference with 350 people at the famous Butlins holiday camp at Bognor Regis. I loved every moment and was surprised at the number of senior managers terrified at the point they were about to go on stage. I taught a few of them this technique literally moments before they were due to start. I learned this presenter state from my trainer, David Shephard. It's written up more fully in his book (written with Tad James) called *Presenting Magically*.

Exercise 42: How to get into the presenter state

Spend a few moments before your next presentation practising these steps. It only takes a few moments.

Step 1: Put any other thoughts or issues out of your mind. For example, if you're worried about the row you had with your partner before you left for work, put it to one side so that you are totally present in this moment and are aware of what is happening around you.

Step 2: Now get physiologically comfortable. You should be standing upright with your energy centred. To do this, bring your attention to the area below your belly button. Relax your hands down by your sides and have your feet shoulder width apart. Make sure you are balanced in your weight distribution and your physiology is symmetrical, i.e. as if you were standing on a pair of scales and each half of you weighs the same and is a mirror image of the other half.

Step 3: Get your breathing under control. Take a deep breath in through your nose and out through your mouth then breathe normally.

Step 4: Now put your awareness inside of yourself for a few moments. Notice what you notice. Focus on the presentation going perfectly.

Step 5: Bring your awareness back outside into the room and find a spot on the wall to focus on. Put all your attention on that spot and while you do that expand your awareness to fill the room. Notice that in your peripheral vision you can see everyone and everything in the room even though you are still focused on that spot. Take your awareness to all four corners of the room, even behind you.

Step 6: Notice that you can see every small movement that your audience makes whilst in this state. Now as you feel at one with the group, bring your eyes down and look at the group.

Step 7: Notice that you can make eye contact with individuals whilst remaining in peripheral vision. That keeps your awareness in the whole room. Notice how everything begins to flow as you feel at one with the room.

Step 8: Now begin....

The presenter state works because going into and staying in peripheral vision keeps the body in a state of *parasympathetic arousal*. This is the 'rest and digest' state and it keeps the body calm. This is the opposite of the state of *sympathetic arousal* or the 'fight or flight' response. This might feel strange at first but keep practising it because it works.

Working with your energy

Energy is the fuel of excellence. Think for a moment of your favourite car. Perhaps it's a beautiful sports car or an exciting 4 × 4. Whatever it is, imagine trying to drive it on the wrong fuel. It wouldn't work. It's the same for our bodies. To be at peak performance we need to maximise our energy levels. The higher your energy level the better you feel, and the better you feel the more astounding your results will be. As a presenter, feeling grounded and appearing grounded to your audience is very important as you look and feel more confident. In the last exercise I showed you how to centre your energy. Here are three exercises that provide a direct experience of using energy, so you'll know how to work more effectively with the energy in your body in future.

Exercise 43: Learning how to utilise your energy

Find a partner and decide who will go first. If it is you, stand on one spot and put your attention in your left ear lobe and imagine all your energy moving to the top of your head and into that ear lobe. Once you are focusing all your energy into your left ear lobe, your partner will *gently* push you on the shoulder. It is likely that you will wobble all over the place. This symbolises how we are normally – rushing from one priority to another with our focus and energy diluted into too many things.

Next, move your focus and all your energy into your lower stomach, just below the navel. Stand upright and imagine your legs feeling absolutely grounded with roots growing through the floor you are standing on. Remember the analogy of the scales we used earlier – i.e. you should have even weight on both legs. Then your partner will push you *gently* again. Notice the difference. How did you feel the second time around? You will have been rooted to the ground and much firmer. It's amazing how quickly we can focus our energy when we know what to do.

Then repeat the exercise, swapping over with your partner.

You can also use this technique if someone asks you a challenging question or you are thrown off balance by some disruption.

As you lose your mental balance, the risk is that you lose your physical balance as well. If you notice this happening to you, just bring your attention back into your centre again, go back into presenter state and check your breathing. Then carry on; it only takes a few seconds to get back on track again. Being physically balanced will help you deal with any situation during your presentation. You'll notice how you feel more confident, stronger and totally grounded. Practise regularly and enjoy the results.

Exercise 44: Improve your focus, improve your result

Here is another example of energy following thought. You'll need to stand up to do this exercise. Find a space where you can move around with your arm outstretched freely. Look forward and stand with your feet apart. Stand rooted to the floor. Now raise one arm horizontally out in front of you with your index finger pointed and gently twist around keeping your arm horizontal until you cannot twist any further (if you put your right arm out, twist to the right and vice versa). Note carefully where your finger is pointing – maybe there's something in the room you can take as a marker. Or if you have someone else with you, ask them to stand as a marker for where your arm got to. Now focus behind you and find a spot beyond where your arm reached the first time. Fix that spot in your mind as you turn back around to face the front again. Twist again, moving your arm as far as it will go. Hold it steady, turn around and see how much further you have moved your arm this time. You will find that you have moved your arm much further the second time around. You may have twisted to way beyond the point you visualised.

This is another great example of the fact that your energy flows to where your attention goes. The result of visualising this action before doing it is that your arm rotates further. It demonstrates that our minds and bodies are linked – they are one system, not two. This exercise clearly indicates that when you really focus on your result, you can improve it enormously. So focusing on your presentation by way of preparation, rehearsal, feedback, etc. will get you a much better result.

Formatting for success

I am about to share with you one of the most useful things I have ever learned. It's called the '4Mat system'.

Why would you want to learn this system? Well, what if you could learn a simple structure that would enable you to put a presentation together in minutes, regardless of the subject? Imagine you meet your CEO in the corridor early one morning. They say to you, 'Can you come and present to the Board on progress with that project of yours?' You say 'yes', thinking it will be at the next meeting in a month's time. Your CEO then says, 'OK, we'll see you in 30 minutes then.' Rather than having a heart attack at this point, the 4Mat system gives you a method for constructing a presentation almost off the cuff. And, if that's not enough, the 4Mat system is also structured to appeal to all learning styles.

What is the 4Mat system all about?

The 4Mat system comes from a study of different learning styles by Bernice McCarthy. She noticed that children in school learned in four different ways. Some children wanted reasons. They were always asking the question 'why'. Some children wanted the facts. They were always asking the question 'what'. Some children wanted to experiment and try things out. They asked the question 'how'. Finally, some children wanted to explore the future consequences of doing something. They asked the question 'what if'. Bernice noticed that most teaching was done only in the 'what' category. Many presentations today also follow this same pattern. The percentages of people in the US falling into each category are shown in the table.

4Mat	Learning style	Percentage
Why?	Discussion	35
What?	Teaching	22
How?	Coaching	18
What if?	Self-discovery	25

In any audience, there will be a mix of preferences. By bringing it down to these four simple, basic questions, answered in the order shown in the table, McCarthy found that motivation to listen and get engaged and learning was maximised. She found that it was by far the best to start with the 'whys' because, until you give people reasons why they should listen to you, they won't engage or listen to the rest of the information. This is a major reason why so many people switch off in presentations today – they are all about the 'what' and nothing else. Then move on to the 'what'. This is because people need the information before going off and doing an exercise or thinking how they might apply something. Then do the 'how'. During a training session this would be the exercises. In a business presentation, it might be about how your audience can implement what you have taught them back in the workplace. Finally, introduce the 'what if'. This explores the consequences of doing or not doing what you have been discussing. Right at the very start you also need to introduce a 'little what' which just sets the frame for the presentation. For example, today we are going to learn about the 4Mat System.

Exercise 45: How to use the 4Mat system

Think about a forthcoming presentation you have diarised or similar. Plan it out using the 4Mat system. Make sure you really hook in your audience with the 'whys' first. This is what really makes the difference.

If you don't have a presentation coming up, find a subject that you'd like to present. This may be at work or outside. Plan an eight-minute presentation using the 4Mat system. That's roughly two minutes on each of the four questions plus a few seconds at the start for the 'little what'.

With either opportunity, practise your presentation even if it's in front of the mirror or the cat. Remember to get into presenter state first, then off you go.

My key learning points

What if you use the 4Mat system?

We spoke at the start of good presenters having an edge in their company. The 4Mat system is very helpful for taking your presentations to the next level. This will enable you stand for all the right reasons! Imagine in the future if the CEO of your business noticed that you were the one whose presentations had made the difference between winning and losing some major new contracts. What would that be worth to you both?

In contrast, if you stick with your current way of doing things and you lose the next major piece of work, you'd never know how much difference the 4Mat system might have made to your performance and to your results. How would you feel about that? So experiment with the technique and notice the improved results that you get.

And for the observant ones amongst you, you'll notice that I used the 4Mat system to explain the 4Mat system!

Satir categories

Have you ever been in a presentation where the presenter's body language has literally been completely over the top so you were left totally distracted by their random movements on the stage? Or maybe you've been at a presentation where the presenter has stood as still as a statue and you've wondered if they were alive or dead? They certainly have not been entertaining. We are going to learn how to be remembered for the 'right' reasons on stage.

One of the big challenges for presenters is what to do with their hands. I was taught on my NLP trainers' course about the Satir postures that give a non-verbal message to your audience. You can use these postures to support your presentation without having to say anything at all. These postures originated in the book, *Peoplemaking* by Virginia Satir. Satir identifies four postures that people often take during the communication process. A fifth posture, the leveller, was added later.

In *Presenting Magically,* David Shephard and Tad James adapt these postures for presenters with the result that each posture will not only trigger a particular state within you, but will also create an associated state in your audience. Here's how you can use them when you wish to get a particular message across:

- **Leveller.** The leveller uses the grounded posture we learned for the presenter state. Your weight is evenly balanced and your hands are palms down and flat. You move your hands from mid-chest downwards and outwards as if you are running your hands across a table top. You stop at the point that your fingers start to turn diagonally outwards. At the same time as you move your hands down and out you also move one leg out as well until your feet

Leveller   Placater   Blamer

Computer   Distractor

Satir Categories

are a little more than shoulder width apart. The leveller is used to non-verbally assert authority. It gives a signal to your audience that you mean business. It's great to use when you have an important point to make, e.g. 'This is the whole point of my presentation today'. You can make it even stronger by using a falling voice tonality at the same time as you do the movement. This posture is great for women as they come across as assertive and powerful.

- **Placater.** The placater, in contrast, holds their palms upwards in an open gesture, often moving upwards with head slightly dipped. The posture suggests helplessness, vunerability. You would only use this if you needed the support of your audience. Use this position with care, as it can suggest weakness. Women especially should use with caution. Many women naturally use this posture unconsciously and it detracts from their confidence during their presentation.

- **Blamer.** The blamer uses an aggressive posture. They step forwards, with arm raised, pointing a finger of blame. If you do use this posture it's important to point above the heads of your audience. It does bring the presentation alive as it introduces energy. Use it sparingly to get important points across, for example, 'There are three points I want you to understand. Point 1…' etc. Used sparingly, it can have a great impact as it also has an element of surprise.

- **Computer.** Using a grounded posture, the computer has one arm across the body with the elbow of the other arm resting on it and the hand holding or balanced under the chin. It is a thoughtful, reasonable and dissociated posture often used by audio digitals. In your presentation you can use it to make you appear studious and thoughtful and it can buy you time if someone asks you a tough question. It is often accompanied by a monotone tonality.

- **Distractor.** Distractor uses total asymmetry with both arms and legs at different angles and at different heights. It is accompanied by a fluctuating tonality. It's good to use if you want the audience to laugh at something. I use it if I make a mistake. For example, I'll say something like 'did she really say that?' and use the distractor at the same time.

You can also adopt these postures when you are sitting down, though they are most powerful when you are standing. The idea is that if you want to use your hands in your presentation you use them with volition with one of these gestures. When you are not using one of these postures your hands should be relaxed by your side. Of course, it never quite works out that way because we all have our idiosyncrasies when presenting. However, if you watch the world-class presenters they use their posture to make a point or else they are just still and very grounded. That's what the Satir categories can achieve for you.

///

Exercise 46: Postures with a purpose

In your next presentation, practise the Satir postures. Work out beforehand which postures best fit with your presentation. For example, if you are pitching for work, the Leveller is the one to go for, maybe with some Computer during questions and a small amount of Distractor when you want to use humour. Then when you come to present, use the postures and notice what happens. Use your sensory acuity to assess the audience's reaction and notice how you feel inside with each different posture. You'll soon recognise the particular Satir posture that you have habitually used from an unconscious level. It's the one that you do most easily. Notice that and then work more on the others for practice.

Write your key learning points below:

///

As Shephard and James write:

'People will be picking up meaning from this non-verbal communication all the time... The body language you use is a really important part of telling the story. Now that you are using this 55% segment of your communication to enhance the 7% verbal content, you will find you are communicating far more effectively. Using the Satir categories will completely transform your presentation.'

Pulling it all together

Let's finish with a few tips for presenters that I've collected over the years and experimented with myself. The most important one for me is that your audience doesn't know what you meant to say....because for every piece of 'important' information you miss your unconscious mind will present you with another nugget even more important. So go easy on yourself.

- **Tip No. 1:** People see master presenters and think they are natural presenters. It's practice that makes perfect. For two years I was an assistant to one of the most senior partners at the consulting firm where I worked. He was renowned for his slick, articulate and humorous presentations. The first time we travelled together, I was surprised to be asked to watch him rehearse the night before a major client presentation over and over again until he was perfect. The following day, the audience was commenting what a natural he was!

- **Tip No. 2:** You've already heard about the NLP principle of 'acting as if'. Here it works if you use it in the context of 'acting as if' you are already a great presenter. The audience will act as if you are too!

- **Tip No. 3:** Be yourself during your presentation. Many presenters don't think it's OK to be themselves. They come across as inauthentic. If you are yourself you will build much better rapport with your group.

- **Tip No. 4:** Be aware of modern business's 'death by powerpoint' syndrome. You might want to use a few slides, but keep these to a minimum. Let your presentation be more spontaneous and use different approaches.

- **Tip No. 5:** Remember that your audience doesn't know what you are intending to cover. They won't know if you miss out a couple of points. Also, if you tell a joke and no-one laughs, act as if you never meant to be funny. Equally, if you mess up be prepared to laugh at yourself. Everyone is naturally funny – you do not need to tell lots of jokes to achieve this.

- **Tip No. 6:** Become a collector of stories that appeal to you. Then use appropriate stories from your collection when you are developing your presentation. Regardless of what you may have been told in the past, you can use stories in business – just make sure that the links are clear to the points you wish to get across to your audience.

- **Tip No. 7:** Model other great presenters. Look back at Chapter 3 to find out how.

Finally, take what you have learned in this chapter and go out there and do it. Take a step out of your comfort zone and really enjoy the results. Always ask for feedback and use it to keep stepping up your performance.

Remember to breathe when you are delivering your next presentation!

12

EXCEEDING CUSTOMER EXPECTATIONS

///

I s it actually possible to keep up with customer expectations?

Some people argue that, whilst it's not hard to exceed customer expectations one, two or even three times, it's very hard to keep on exceeding customer expectations. This is because customer expectations are constantly going up and up. With every good experience your customer has at one of your competitors, their benchmark of good service levels increases. So your competitor's actions have just as much of an inflationary effect on customer expectations as your own. In fact, your customers are also going to look at their satisfaction with you versus other companies that they interact with. And don't think this just happens with private businesses. There is also a similar effect in the public sector. For example, I was consulting with a team of planners from a seaside Borough Council. Their planning processes were outdated compared to other planning authorities. In particular, their website was unable to process planning applications on-line, unlike most of the surrounding local authorities who had made the necessary investment in new systems. This caused major irritations for customers moving into the area from neighbouring boroughs because they expected at least the same level of service that they had enjoyed elsewhere.

So why bother?

You will learn from the Vue cinema chain case study in this chapter that there's always an opportunity to stand out from the crowd. It's no different in the public sector where audit commission ratings are a matter of organisational pride and bring in the best staff wanting to work for the public sector organisations with the best reputations. Exceeding expectations keeps our existing customer base returning to us time and time again. This saves time and money in marketing and sales to new customers and it builds long-term rapport with each customer. For example, success for me is a new customer attending my 3-hour NLP taster session who then goes on to attend the NLP Practitioner and Master Practitioner programmes and is knocking on my office door wanting to know what else they can go on. I know then that I have succeeded. Excellent customer service also motivates staff. Firstly, because when customers are happy, staff have fewer complaints and 'difficult' customers to deal with. Secondly, staff are more likely to be motivated by the authority they have been given to resolve potential issues at the point of contact. Finally, they are at the leading edge of new ideas and opportunities. This is inspiring for many staff. All of these points mean improved results for your business.

NLP helps because it teaches us to focus on being the best by setting clear goals and continually increasing our standards, learning from feedback until we become world-class at what we do. It's an ongoing journey of continuous improvement to be the best that we can be. That's why, if you're serious about NLP, it's impossible to settle for second best. As NLPers we are continually searching for more creative ways of serving our customers because excellent customer service differentiates us from the pack. Everything you've learned so far in this book about NLP will assist you to exceed your customer's expectations – especially all the tools in the last two chapters. Now we'll discover how to pull these ideas together so we can hit the ground running.

What are your experiences?

Let's start by exploring how you have had your expectations exceeded as a customer. These can be from any area of your life – or from your business. For example, this week I had two contrasting examples of customer service. The first involved two phone calls in two days from my private health insurer wanting to check with me before renewing my policy for another year. In principle that was good customer service. However, on day 1 they called me in the middle of my working day. I told them it wasn't convenient to speak but I would like to go through a few things so could they call back after 6pm that same evening. They said of course they would – but there was no phone call. The next day the same thing happened. I had a call during the day. I explained that I had asked for an evening call the day before which hadn't happened. There was no apology; the operator only said, 'We can't do that, I'm afraid, as there's no field in the system to record when to call you back'.

Then I felt irritated and they haven't called back at all since. The next day one of their competitors called me about private health care and I asked them for a quote. I wouldn't have done that 24 hours earlier.

The second customer service experience involved me calling a well-known car insurance site to get a quote for my 17-year-old son to drive his first car. The woman was very helpful and was almost apologetic when she told me the cost. She even went away to discuss it with the underwriters to get a better deal for me. However, the quote she obtained was still too high and I told her that I would call some other companies. She empathised with me and asked if it would be ok for her to call me at 6pm that night to see how I'd got on. I told her that was fine. At 6pm on the dot, she called me and I explained I had found a cheaper quote. She wished me luck and asked if I would think of them next time I was searching for insurance. I told her that I definitely would.

Two very different scenarios: the first with ineffective systems and staff making excuses; the second with staff who did as they promised, were focused on my needs and were very helpful. If we think back to the principles of 'results vs reasons' and 'cause vs effect (Chapter 2), the first company did not take personal responsibility for the situation and did not do whatever it took to solve it for me. Instead, the first customer service representative said they would call me at 6pm that evening and didn't, followed by the second, who just made excuses by focusing on the 'reasons' why calling me at a specific time was impossible anyway due to their inefficient systems. The second company representative built great rapport with me, took 100% responsibility for doing the best they could for me and kept their agreement despite the fact that it was very unlikely they'd make the deal with me. That representative definitely exceeded my expectations to the extent that I will call them next time I need some insurance.

When I reflected on the calls later I realised there were important lessons and reminders for me as a business owner:

- Keep your agreements with customers
- Apologise when things go wrong
- Take personal responsibility for making things happen

- Build empathy with your customer

- Ask for feedback on the spot

- Build loyalty for the future

Not exactly rocket science yet how many businesses need reminding about these basic principles? Does yours?

Exercise 47: Your personal experiences of having your expectations exceeded

Now it's your turn. Make a note below of one or two examples of exceptional customer service you have received recently and the lessons for your business:

Examples of exceptional customer service:

Lessons for my business:

I particularly enjoy discovering examples of creativity and exceeding expectations in what appears to the rest of the world to be a crowded market place. Consider VUE cinemas...

Turning 'vueing' on its head

(from an article by Helen Dunne called 'Vue Cinemas have a fresh take on film-going', Telegraph.co.uk 20.01.09)

Almost 13 years ago, Canadian-born lawyer Tim Richards spent two years in an office above his garage in Hollywood Hills, working out the blueprint for his business venture. In 2008, Vue Cinemas, the company born above that garage, celebrated its 10th anniversary while its 65 cinemas, stretching from Inverness to the south coast, served almost 35 million customers – roughly 20 per cent of the market – and generating revenues of £250m. Vue has gone from strength to strength, opening new sites and outperforming the industry. Mr Richards also funded a management buy-out with a package of debt and equity, which allows him and his team to take control of their own destiny.

Mr Richards' ethos was always to 'shake things up a little'. He is continuously testing and innovating and believes that research is the key to their success. They often test new initiatives out on a small number of cinemas before rolling out across the whole group. For example, many cinemas now have comfortable leather seats in three rows of the auditorium and a licensed bar because research revealed that customers wanted these facilities. Richards argues that many innovations do not cost a lot to implement but they take creativity and imagination to give them a go.

An example of an unexpected innovation took place shortly after the release of the popular 'Mamma Mia!' A

Vue executive held a private screening and inadvertently left the subtitle facility on. 'It was a genuine mistake. All films have subtitle options for the hard of hearing.' explains Mr Richards. 'But his friends treated it as a karaoke-style experience, and the press caught on.' Vue soon launched the singalong concept. It gave 'Mamma Mia!' another lease of life and Vue is planning to bring it back every year

How do you get started?

There are some very definite lessons in this case study for the rest of us. First of all, research what your customers want and get feedback. Then pilot in a few places to thoroughly test the concept before full roll-out. Finally, do what you can to take 100% responsibility for sorting out a customer's problem – being in control of your own destiny leads to a more agile customer services team. Let's explore this in more detail.

Step 1: Find out what your customer wants

In order to exceed customer expectations you have to know what their expectations are in the first place. In the moment, unless the salesperson specifically asks the customer what they expect and want to happen during the sale, they will never know. Most of the time, salespeople, like the company, often arrogantly assume they know what the customer wants and asking seems to be a waste of time. Not until they have experienced the variety of expectations that different customers have will they appreciate the need for the question. When asked about their expectations, customers are surprised as more than likely they have never been asked this question before. The salesperson may have to ask a couple of questions to get the customer on track. The following example questions will help your salespeople get started – use the ones that best fit your business and develop some of your own:

- What's most important to you about this application/ purchase/booking?

- How often would you like me to keep you informed about progress?

- How/when would you prefer I contact you?

- If I need to get hold of you at short notice and you are not available, is there an alternative individual I may speak with?

- Are you going to need any additional assistance from us when we deliver?

- Have I missed anything?

If the salesperson has done a thorough job in discovering the client's expectations and needs, they know exactly what they must do in order to give the customer the best possible purchasing experience. This is similar to the experience I had with the car insurance saleswoman. This discussion of the customer's expectations also allows the salesperson to manage any unrealistic expectations the customer may have at this early stage.

Step 2: Get ahead of the game

In the longer term, research about customer expectations is equally important. We saw in the Vue case study how this is central to their success. This can be part of the feedback process (see Step 3) though it's likely to be a wider exercise that models what your competitors are doing as well as asking your potential customers about their expectations for the future. It's very easy these days to canvas opinions about important issues. With newsletter and survey software freely available you can canvas the opinions of your customers much more easily than in the past. You can also lodge a question on your website and gather views that way. It's also easy to surf the web sites of your key competitors and to sign up to their newsletters and free materials to find out what they are up to on the customer front. Social media also makes it easy these days to reach large numbers of potential new customers. These are all low-cost options. Marketing companies are also available to run larger-scale research projects for bigger businesses.

As an example of a research opportunity, The Change Corporation is currently undertaking a piece of academic research with Dr Julie Hodges from Durham Business School on the status of mid-life business women. (40–60 years old), either running their own company or working for one. The research paper will be published and seeks to answer questions along the lines of 'What status do mid-life women have in the business world'. The results will be used to inform my Age with Attitude personal development programme for mid-life women. I put together a proposal, similar to a basic business case for the research. Julie and I drafted the survey together through a number of iterations and then transferred into survey software. The survey has been sent out to a number of databases and women's business networking groups. We are currently awaiting the results which will be analysed and then published. This is a great opportunity for us to work in partnership and share our expertise for a relatively small cost.

Step 3: Ask for feedback

Take the initiative to ask for feedback of any sort, and respond to it quickly. If someone takes the time to compliment your organisation, thank them immediately. If they offer you areas for improvement, thank them immediately. Respond quickly and decisively. Exceed their expectations. Here's a small example. The other day a customer called our office to complain that they hadn't been sent some information about a course that they were expecting. I not only sent them the information they wanted, I also sent them a free DVD (normally retailing at £29.99) by special delivery to apologise and thank them for helping us to tighten up our processes. They called the office two days later and booked onto our flagship 7 Day Fast Track NLP Practitioner programme.

Take any feedback as a gift as it will enable you to take your business to the next level. We ask for written feedback on all of our training programmes – even free sessions. We also invite feedback through our regular newsletters. This feedback has helped us to transform our business model over the last five years.

Step 4: Give authority

Each of your salespeople must have the authority, within reasonable limits, to be able to respond to customer requests. The decisions of salespeople must then be upheld by their managers. This, unfortunately, is where it gets difficult for larger companies. Not only are larger companies reluctant to give salespeople the authority to make things happen, their processes and procedures are so inflexible that it is almost impossible for any customisation to take place. Yet, the inflexibility of the large company and its reluctance to delegate authority opens tremendous doors for smaller companies. These have the flexibility and willingness to empower their salespeople to make the changes to the way they do business, ensuring their customers do have a one-of-a-kind buying experience.

As mentioned above, not every expectation by a customer can be met by even the most agile of companies. Nevertheless, the more flexible and accommodating the company can be and the more authority it can give to salespeople to work with customers, the more impressive the impact the company's service will have on the customer. In many cases, if the salesperson knows what the client's expectations really are and

A win-win scenario

The recession has meant many of our customers at The Change Corporation have had to tighten their belts. We have responded by offering interest-free payment plans – it's a win–win situation because our customers can still come along and we get our classes filled. It was a financial challenge in the beginning to set this up but now it provides a regular income for us. There are very few NLP companies in the UK offering this facility so we know we are exceeding expectations on this one.

can truly exceed them, price becomes a non-issue, as does the competition.

Exercise 48: Getting started with your customers

This exercise is all about discovering what your customers think about your business. You will need to devise a strategy for finding out more about their expectations and getting feedback. Use Steps 1–4 to help you. Surveys, feedback forms and focus groups are all great channels for gaining information. We have run focus groups in the past of people in our target customer groups. We've found that they are willing to help as long as they get something in return – such as discount vouchers, nice lunch and drinks at the meeting, etc.

Here are some example questions to get you started:

- Why did they select your business?
- What's the most important to them about their own customer experience?
- What other things are also important?
- What do they value about the products and/or services you provide?

- What do you not provide that they would like?
- What have been the highs of their customer experience with you?
- What have been the lows of their customer experience with you?
- What would cause them to move to another supplier?

What did you learn from gathering this feedback?

What new standards for customer service would you like to set as a result?

Pulling it all together

At one time, the myth of exceeding the customer's expectations was all powerful. Today, as more and more companies claim to give more than the customer expects it's becoming increasingly harder to keep up. Yet there are still amazing opportunities to find a new approach to an old situation – take Vue as an example. In this fast new world of social media, news travels fast and old formulas need to be challenged and changed. The good news is that businesses willing to step outside their comfort zones to learn about their customers and then to institute the changes necessary are finding themselves without competition and are able to maintain their pricing structure in the face of ever-declining prices from competitors.

TIP *Treat any feedback as a gift. Your business and you won't be disappointed.*

ARE YOU READY?

D on't blame me if, as a result of reading this book, you begin to create the changes you want in your business. This journey has taken you through four different yet related territories: personal leadership, team performance, organisational change and customer excellence. You now have a massive NLP toolkit to transform your results. I feel like Trinity in 'The Matrix' as I have been plugged in for several months now downloading the contents of my brain into this book for you to take away and use as a pragmatic 'how-to' manual for creating the type of business success you have only dared to dream about up until now.

NLP – An art and a science

I chose NLP as the toolkit for this journey because it is the most results-focused technology I have ever come across – it focuses on solutions and not problems. That doesn't mean that you can't 'mix it' with other useful tools that you have discovered – you can. The important question to keep in mind is 'which technology will get me to my result fastest?' For me, in nine cases out of ten, this has meant using NLP. Sometimes a client asks me to use NLP explicitly, for example, in an NLP Business Practitioner. At other times, they want the tools more covertly as part of a wider leadership, team development or customer services initiative. It doesn't matter how NLP is presented, the most important element that makes it so successful for change at work is that it works. I've often heard people asking whether NLP is an art or a science. In my personal view it is *both*. NLP has the benefit of the structure and rigour of science and the creativity of art.

There's no doubt that NLP is process driven. That's why there are so many exercises in this book – 49 of them to be precise. This takes the risk out of change for you, the practitioner. You apply a specific process in a specific way and you can expect a specific result. That's why it's good for high-risk transformation work as it uses both system and process to deliver. So, if you systematically go through the exercises in this book you will get different results. I guarantee that. On the other hand, one of the most important principles of NLP is around flexibility. So if what you are doing doesn't work, do something different. This involves being creative around how you use NLP. Be curious and experiment with your modelling projects and play around with the processes in this book – who knows, you may develop some new patterns of NLP and be able to write about them yourself. So NLP is a nice contradiction in terms and we have to learn to balance both elements. I take comfort in the advice I was given by my NLP trainer and mentor – you just keep going until you achieve your goals. If something works, do more of it. If it doesn't, change it fast!

How much have you learned about NLP?

I told you at the beginning of this book that we were going to cover many core elements of NLP. Some of these are 'traditional' NLP such as modelling and the meta and Milton language patterns. Others, such as cause and effect, were added later by great exponents of NLP like Tad James. Appendix 1 sets out all 33 of the tools and where they appear in this book. These tools are taken from the curriculum of both the NLP Practitioner and Master Practitioner programmes. If you want to find out more visit the web site of the American Board of NLP at www.abh-abnlp.com and review the standards for each programme. If I've inspired you to become a Certified

Practitioner or Master Practitioner of NLP then visit the section at the end of this book called 'What Next?' to discover how to do just that.

If you're serious about your NLP journey you'll want to find out just how much you've learned. In Appendix 3, I've included a multiple choice exercise to check out your knowledge. It's a light-hearted way of you discovering how far you've come already. I'd also advise you to go back to the start of this book and re-take the 'Business Discovery Quiz' in the Introduction. Discover how much you've improved your scores! Have fun with them both as you realise how far you've come.

My Personal Action Plan

My goal has been to inspire you to think and feel differently about your future as a leader. To discover what is possible and to really go for what you want in your business. Throughout this book I have been able to give you ideas, skills, tools and the motivation to change your leadership style and your business. To really go for what you want. Now as you are nearing the end you have a choice to make. This is one of those moments of truth. If you buy a beautiful new wardrobe and leave it in the box because you can't quite work out how to put it together, it's a waste of your effort and investment in buying it in the first place. Learning is like that too. If you have devoured the NLP techniques in this book yet you have no intention of utilising them for your own development or that of your business or your staff you have wasted your energy. All you will do is to slide back quietly into the Grey Zone.

On the other hand, you can unpack the box and begin to move to the 'cause-side' of the equation to nurture those powerful beliefs that will create what you want and move you towards the Brilliant Zone. How do you feel about taking that first step?

Are you ready?

Change leads to more change. Every step you take brings a success that will inspire you to make the next move. You've learned that the most important thing is to keep going until you reach your goal. Remember there is no failure, only feedback. Let's use the last exercise to pull together your own Personal Change Plan for the next twelve months.

///

Exercise 49: My Personal Change Plan

Step 1: Go back through all the exercises you completed in this book and list below the top 10 things you want to change – whether this is about your leadership vision, your team, your organisation or your customers. Remember you're focusing on the next 12 months.

Step 2: Then begin to sort them into the following time line:

2a. Things you can get started on immediately

2b. Things you will achieve within the next month

2c. Things you will achieve within the next 3 months

2d. Things you will have achieved within the next 6 months

2e. Things you will have achieved within the next year

Step 3: Be your own coach - rate your level of motivation to achieve these things from 1-10 (with 10 being high):

Step 4: If your level of motivation is 7 or less ask yourself this question: 'What else needs to happen to raise this willingness to 8 or above?' Make a note below:

Step 5: Commitment to Me!

I commit to doing whatever it takes for me to achieve these actions for change. I do this with passion and excitement for the future.

Signed:

Visualising your success

Imagine yourself in a year's time having made all the changes you have committed to making. Notice what thoughts that image conjures up in your mind. What are you seeing yourself doing, hearing yourself saying and how are you feeling? Close your eyes if it helps to get a clearer image. Make sure that you are looking through your own eyes in the image that you have as opposed to seeing yourself in the picture. That makes the effect much more powerful. Notice how you can turn up the brightness of everything around you. Pretend that your mind works like a television set and you can adjust the brightness and colour controls. What sounds are associated with your image? Again, turn up the volume control on your TV set and hear what others are saying about you and what you are saying to yourself. Notice the feelings that your thoughts create inside you and turn up those feelings to double or triple intensity. You can do this by just turning your attention onto where those feelings are located in your body. Notice as well, if those feelings are moving around. If they are, make them move faster and notice how this intensifies them. How does that feel? Did you notice the feelings in your image becoming more intense?

Now step out of the image you have created so now you see yourself in the image. Visualise for a few minutes each day, stepping into the 'you' of 12 months time who has achieved everything you set to do, be and have. Turn up the colours, brightness, sounds and feelings to send a clear and strong message to your unconscious mind that you are serious about the changes you wish to make. Have fun with this and play around until you find a perfect combination for increasing your mental imagery.

My final words...

I hope that I've inspired you to do something different – to move out of the Grey Zone towards the Brilliant Zone. That's where I'm heading and I'd like to meet up with you there. Here are my final thoughts about NLP that will move you forwards. First, know what you want. In any situation, have a clear outcome of what you want to achieve. Second, be aware and alert. Have sufficient sensory awareness of yourself and others to know when you are moving towards or away from your outcome. Third, have sufficient flexibility to be able to keep changing your behaviour until you get your outcome. Finally, take action *now* and remember that anything less than 100% effort is sabotage!

Enjoy the journey.

What Next?

I know that some of you will want to take your learning about NLP further either for you individually or for your organisation.

Here are the services we offer.

Corporate Services

Learning and development

We use NLP in our work to deliver performance improvement for our customers. We offer bespoke in-house programmes to meet your specific requirements in the areas of change management, leadership development, team building and wellbeing. We also offer training needs analysis services.

Executive coaching

We provide customised coaching interventions and we specialise in coaching senior female executives.

Change management consultancy

We can advise and assist you to manage the 'people side' of change, building staff commitment, capability and minimising resistance.

Culture change

We can advise you how to achieve long-term culture change in your business and assist you to deliver behavioural change.

Public programmes

Powerful presentations

A 3-day programme that uses NLP to build your confidence and beliefs as a presenter. We teach you how to present with charisma in any situation and get the results you want.

7-day fast track NLP Practitioner, Practitioner of Time Line Therapy™ and Practitioner of Hypnotherapy

You will learn how to use NLP techniques to transform your own life and help others. Our Practitioner programme allows you to become a Certified Practitioner of NLP in seven days. We do this by utilising pre-study CDs that you will then be able to use as a useful refresher long after the training has finished. You will also study to become a Practitioner of Time Line Therapy™ and a Practitioner of Hypnosis.

14-day fast track NLP Master Practitioner, Master Practitioner of Time Line Therapy™ and Master Hypnotist

Our Master Practitioner programme will not only enable you to take your practitioner skills to a mastery level, but it will also teach you many advanced techniques. You will also have the opportunity to become a Master Practitioner of Time Line Therapy™ and a Master Hypnotist. This programme also has a pre-study component.

Age with Attitude™

This is a unique personal development programme for midlife women, and it's the first of its kind. It is a 10-month journey spread across four events, with coaching and assistance in between each event to help keep you on track to achieve your goals. You work with other like-minded women who will support and inspire you to create the life that you want.

BreakThrough coaching

We offer a fast-track way of dealing with long-term limiting patterns of behaviour. We work intensively together for one day to resolve a particular issue with follow-up assistance.

Free buddy service

This service is designed to 'buddy' our readers to work together to achieve their outcomes. All you have to do is email or call us, and we'll let you know if we have anyone available to work with you. We put you in touch and then it's over to you.

If you would like more information on NLP or the courses available from The Change Corporation, send an email to info@ thechangecorporation.com or visit our websites:

www.thechangecorporation.com

www.lindseyagness.com

www.agewithattitude.co.uk

APPENDIX 1:
NLP GRID

///

	Tools	Strategies for Success	Winning State of Mind	Modelling World-Class Performance	Constructing High Performing Teams
1	Goal setting	X			
2	Well formed outcomes	X			
3	Principles of success	X			
4	Grey Zone	X			
5	Pre-suppositions of NLP		X		
6	NLP frames		X		
7	Communications model		X		
8	Belief change		X		
9	Focus on what you want		X		
10	Modelling			X	
11	Meta programmes				X
12	Values elicitation				X

	Tools	Encouraging Creativity	Courageous Conversations	Managing Change Effectively	Changing the ROTG
13	Anchoring	X			
14	Hierarchy of ideas	X			
15	NLP feedback sandwich		X		
16	NLP coaching model		X		
17	Meta model			X	
18	Milton model			X	
19	Embedded commands			X	
20	Perceptual positions			X	
21	Neurological or logical Levels of change			X	
22	Pattern break				X
23	Strategies and TOTE				X

	Tools	Developing Global orgs	Influencing With Integrity	Powerful Presentations	Are You Ready?
24	Impact of communication	X			
25	New meta pro-grammes	X			
26	Rapport		X		
27	Sensory acuity		X		
28	Representational systems		X		
29	Eye patterns		X		
30	Presenter state			X	
31	4Mat system (as adapted for NLP)			X	
32	Satir categories			X	
33	Visualisation				X

APPENDIX 2:

THE LANGUAGE USED BY DIFFERENT REPRESENTATIONAL SYSTEMS

Visual	Kinaesthetic	Auditory	Audio digital
see	feel	hear	sense
look	touch	listen	experience
appear	grasp	sound(s)	understand
view	get hold of	make music	think
show	slip through	harmonise	learn
dawn	catch on	tune in/out	process
reveal	tap into	be all ears	decide
envision	make contact	rings a bell	motivate
illuminate	throw out	silence	consider
twinkle	turn around	be heard	change
clear	hard	resonate	perceive
foggy	unfeeling	deaf	insensitive
focussed	concrete	mellifluous	distinct
hazy	scrape	dissonance	conceive
crystal clear	get a handle on	overtones	know

(Continued)

Visual	Kinaesthetic	Auditory	Audio digital
flash	solid	unhearing	question
imagine	suffer	attune	be conscious
picture	unbudging	outspoken	logic
sparkling	impression	tell	reasonable
snap shot	touch base	announce	statistically
vivid	rub	talk	
perceive	smooth	speak	
light	pushy	resonate	
ray	stumble	state	
mesmerise	in touch	whine	
watch	relaxed	babble	
perspective	loose	echo	
frame	cool	orchestrate	
shine	tepid	whisper	
dim	heavy	snap	
image		hum	
vision		loud	
observe		dialogue	

Used with permission Copyright © The Tad James Co, Tad and Adriana James

Appendix 3:
What have you Learned about NLP?

1. **Which of these is not a core principle of NLP?**

   (a) Everyone has a different model of the world

   (b) There is no failure only feedback

   (c) The toughest will always get the best results

2. **Which of these statements is by someone on the 'effect' side of the equation?**

   (a) I take responsibility for whatever happens in my life

   (b) It's not my fault you didn't get your promotion as I did make a request to HR

   (c) I'm going to adopt a different strategy this time

3. **Learnings are always:**

   (a) For you, positive and for the future

   (b) Good things to have

   (c) What you give to others

4. **What happens if you take 100% responsibility for what you want?**

(a) You'll always have someone to blame

(b) You'll achieve your goals

(c) You can tell others what to do

5. What is your reticular activating system?

(a) Secret weapon

(b) Another word for goals

(c) Filter between our conscious and unconscious minds

6. What do we not model?

(a) External behaviour

(b) Internal emotional state

(c) accent

7. Which meta programme describes how you deal with feedback?

(a) Direction filter

(b) Relationship filter

(c) Frame of reference filter

8. Perceivers like to:

(a) Live in a very orderly way

(b) Keep their options open

(c) Know when they've made the right decision

9. Why are shared values important for a high performing team?

(a) Members are aligned

(b) Useful for appraisal meetings

(c) Helps to set goals

10. Which NLP technique helps with lateral thinking?

(a) Mind-maps

(b) Chunking up and down the 'Hierarchy of Ideas'

(c) Global meta programme

11. **What question do we use to get more abstract answers?**

(a) What are examples of this?

(b) What is this an example of?

(c) What specifically?

12. **In a coaching session the coach will talk:**

(a) Most of the time

(b) No more than 40% of the time

(c) No more than 25% of the time

13. **What is the meta model?**

(a) Questions to recover generalisations, deletions and distortions in language

(b) Way of understanding other models of the world

(c) Bandler and Grinder's fourth language model

14. **How would you challenge a cause and effect violation?**

(a) Why do you think that?

(b) How does what they have done cause you to choose to feel…?

(c) What does this mean?

15. **How would you finish this tag question: 'you know this…?'**

(a) Don't you?

(b) You really do?

(c) I can tell?

16. **How would you describe a nominalisation?**

(a) An abstract noun

(b) A word that you can put into a wheel barrow

(c) A number

17. **Which of these is incorrect?**

    (a) Test – here we set or access the criteria for the 'desired state'

    (b) Operate – here we gather data

    (c) Exit – here we always exit first time

18. **What impact do our words have in our communication?**

    (a) 7%

    (b) 10%

    (c) 15%

19. **'if I said 'you should have arranged with that customer when to call them back' would I be speaking:**

    (a) Literally

    (b) Inferentially

    (c) Specifically

20. **Which should you not match when building rapport using your voice?**

    (a) Tempo

    (b) Accent

    (c) Tone

21. **Which best describes a visual communicator?**

    (a) Thin and wiry

    (b) Processes information through pictures

    (c) Like to get close to the action

22. **If you are reverse organised what does it mean?**

    (a) You write with your left hand

    (b) Your eye patterns are reversed

    (c) You spend most of your time in your thoughts

23. What's the order of the 4Mat system?

  (a) Why, what, how, what if

  (b) How, why, what, what if

  (c) Little what, why, what, how, what if

24. Which Satir category is best for women?

  (a) Placater

  (b) Blamer

  (c) Leveller

25. Which NLP technique is best for customer service?

  (a) Rapport

  (b) Sensory acuity

  (c) Language patterns (i.e. Milton and meta)

Answers

1 (c) 2 (b) 3 (a) 4 (b) 5 (c) 6 (c) 7 (c) 8 (b) 9 (a) 10 (b) 11 (b) 12 (b) 13 (a) 14 (b) 15 (a) 16 (a) 17 (c) 18 (a) 19 (a) 20 (b) 21 (b) 22 (b) 23 (c) 24 (c) 25 all of them! (3 points)

Scores

You score one point per correct answer

  22–27 points: Well done! You have really focussed on learning your NLP. You are on your way towards the Brilliant Zone.

  15–22 points: An average score. If you want to step up your game in business go back to the appropriate chapters and find the right answers.

  Less than 15: A below average score. If you want to be remembered in business for the right reasons start again and re-read the book, this time paying more attention to the NLP tools and techniques.

BIBLIOGRAPHY

Agness, Lindsey, *Change Your Life with NLP*, Pearson 2008

Bonthos, J.M. 'Culture – The missing intelligence variable, *The Strategic Planning News*, March 1994

Bostic St Clair, Carmen and Grinder, John, *Whispering in the Wind*, J & C Enterprises 2001

Branson, Richard, *Screw It, Let's Do It*, Virgin Books 2006

Charvet, Shelle Rose, *Words that Change Minds*, Kendall Hunt Publishing 1997

Covey, Stephen, *Seven Habits of Highly Effective People*, Simon & Schuster 1989

Csikszentmihalyi, Mihaly, *Flow: The classic work on how to achieve happiness*, Random House 2002

Dilts, Robert, *Changing Belief Systems with NLP*, Meta Publications 1990

Dilts, Robert, *Strategies of Genius*, Meta Publications 1991

Goldsmith, Marshall, *What Got You Here Won't Get You There*, Profile Books 2008

Hiatt, Jeffrey M. and Creasey, Timothy J., *Change Management: The people side of change*, Prosci 2003

James, Tad and Shephard, David, *Presenting Magically*, Crown House Publishing 2001

James, Tad and Woodsmall, Wyatt, *Time Line Therapy and the Basis of Personality*, Meta Publications 1988

Knight, Sue, *NLP at Work*, Nicholas Brealey Publishing, 2004

Koppel, Robert, *The Intuitive Trader*, John Wiley & Sons 1996

Korzybski, Alfred, *Science and Sanity*, Institute of General Semantics 1995

Laborde, Genie Z., *Influencing with Integrity*, Crown House Publishing 2009

Lewis, Byron and Pucelik, Frank. *Magic of NLP De-Mystified*, Metamorphous Press 1990

Mehrabian, A. *Silent Messages*, 2nd revised edition, Wadsworth Publishing Co Inc 1981

Mankins, Michael C. and Steele, Richard, *Turning Strategy into Great Performance*, HBR 2005

McDonald, Larry and Robinson, Patrick, *A Colossal Failure of Common Sense*, Ebury 2009

McGuiness, Mark, The Secret of Walt Disney's Creativity, lateralaction.com, 4 May 2009

Meyer, Paul J, *Attitude is Everything* (Attitude & Motivation Vol. 2), published by Paul J Meyer, date unknown

Paulson, Hank, *On the Brink*, Headline Publishing Group 2010

Pritchett, Price and Pound, Ron, *High Velocity Culture Change: A handbook for managers*, Pritchett LLC

Prosci Benchmarking Report, *Best Practices in Change Management*, Prosci 2009

Robbins, Anthony, *Awaken the Giant Within*, Simon & Schuster 1991

Satir, Virginia. *People Making*, Science & Behaviour Books 1972

Senge, Peter M, *The Fifth Discipline*, Random House Publishing 1990

Tosey, Paul and Mathison, Jane, *Neuro-Linguistic Programming: A critical appreciation for managers and developers*, Palgrave Macmillan 2009

About the author

Lindsey Agness is the best-selling author of *Change Your Life with NLP* and *Still 25 Inside* and an experienced NLP trainer. She began her career in local government before becoming a change consultant for one of the top global firms in 1994. There she learned about the art of people change both from an organisational and individual level. She started her NLP journey in 1997 when she wanted to improve her own performance in meetings with large numbers of grey-suited men. In 2005, she founded The Change Corporation. She now spends her time consulting on change projects, coaching senior executives, running open NLP programmes and public speaking. She is well-respected for getting results and improving performance. She also loves to write and enjoys the opportunity to share her insights and experiences with larger audiences. Her personal vision is to become a leader in the development field and to assist organisations and individuals to perform at their highest level.

Originally from the East End of London, she now lives in Sandwich with her two children, Sophie and Oliver.

www.thechangecorporation.com

Acknowledgements

To

My parents who are always there to help me out
My amazing children who give me their encouragement
and love
My partner Jonny who supports and nurtures me to be the
best I can be
My girlfriends – you know who you are
The staff at Capstone Wiley, especially Holly Bennion and
Jenny Ng and Grace O'Byrne.
Graham Maw Christie and especially to Jane
David Shephard, Tad James and Robert Smith for opening
the door to a new world for me!
Diagrams by Billie Burvill (www.billieburvill.co.uk)
Author photo by Paul Webb (www.pwebb.co.uk)
And all those who have endorsed the book for me.
Names of individuals in case studies have been changed.

INDEX